D0065223

After the terror

To Ingrid

After the terror

TED HONDERICH

EDINBURGH UNIVERSITY PRESS

© Ted Honderich, 2002

Edinburgh University Press Ltd
22 George Square, Edinburgh

Typeset in Linotype Palatino
by Koinonia, Manchester, and
printed and bound in Great Britain
by The Bath Press, Bath

A CIP record for this book is available from the British Library

ISBN 0 7486 1667 5 (hardback)

The right of Ted Honderich to be identified as author
of this work has been asserted in accordance with
the Copyright, Designs and Patents Act 1988.

Contents

Contents

Acknowledgements

Thanks to Shahrar Ali, Michael Berkowitz, Ingrid Coggin Purkiss, James Der Derian, Elizabeth and Thomas Fortescue Hitchins, James Garvey, Mark Geller, Anna Ghonim, Jude Harris, Beland Honderich, Kiaran Honderich, Ruth Honderich Spielbergs, Jackie Jones, Ed Kent, Mark Lovas, William McBride, Saladin Meckled-Garcia, Ada Rapoport-Albert, Steven Rose, Richard Rosen, Mary Warnock and Noam Zohar. None is incriminated by having read the manuscript or a part. None agrees with it all. Do some agree with none of it?

1
Good lives, bad lives

Living longer

What is a good life? For a start, a good life is one that goes on long enough. A short life may be good while it lasts, may be a sweet thing in the memory of others. But if it is only half the length it should have been, if it is cut down to that, it is not a good life. A good life might be as long as one you know that comes back to mind, maybe like the life of my father, who departed during his afternoon nap. It might be seventy-five years.

Lasting seventy-five years, of course, cannot by itself make a life a good one. If it was filled with disappointments, let alone dragged down by sorrows or defeats, it would not have been a good life. You can do more than wonder if some lives would have been better if they had been shorter, not prolonged. Some are rightly shortened by their owners. Each of us ought in the end to have the right in morality and law of ending our existence.

So how long a life goes on does not by itself make it a good one. But is there a mistake in saying that living long enough is one part of a good life? No, living longer is a good thing for almost everyone. This is shown by the fact that a life may not be a good one at all but very likely will be better than nothing to its owner. Whatever thought an aged aunt reveals, maybe that she's had a full life and a good time and doesn't mind departing, almost all of us want to go on in a life. This is, isn't it, our first and then our constant and then our last desire? Some call it the instinct of self-preservation. Few of us are so unfortunate as ever really to prefer not being alive. Almost all of us want to go on even if things are bad, even terrible. Hardly anyone chooses to be *missing*.

Can we then say that living longer is an intrinsic good for almost everyone – that is, something good in itself rather than as a means to something else? So it seems, certainly if we take living in our ordinary way. It is not just being alive, as a plant is alive. Nor is it just the idea of being conscious, of there being a personal world, although that is essential and important. Rather, the idea we have of living includes some elementary satisfaction having to do with *existing* rather than just being conscious, maybe the satisfaction of taking things in and watching them change, and conducting small matters of daily life, and having the hope of going on in this way for a while.

This is not the different and more ambitious thing we have in mind in ordinarily speaking of wanting the quality of our lives to be good, wanting a better quality of life. Maybe that has to do with getting a summer cottage, or one on a better lake. But just going on living, living longer, is certainly more than desirable. If it does need to be distinguished from much else that we also want, it is indeed for almost all of us an intrinsic good. We want it for itself, whether or not it is a means to anything else. The ancient Greek philosopher Epicurus tells us not to worry about death, because it itself isn't experienced – where you are, your death isn't, and where it is, you aren't. Only impressionable logicians are consoled.

Living longer isn't a small or smaller intrinsic good idea either, like feeling the warm sun on your shoulders or a happy conversation or having something off your mind after a couple of years. It's a very large thing, so large that you can say this elementary living-of-a-life, in the absence of anything else, can fill a mind, fill a life. We want it a lot. We fight for it, usually quietly. It is not only an intrinsic but a *great good*.

Being rational, at least in this matter, we in a way want something else as much. This is the means to the end, the means to living longer. The means to living longer are shelter, satisfactory food and drink, health, safety and the like, not too much real stress and strain. Part of their importance, if not all, is that they are necessary means if I am to avoid that alternative to living that is nothing at all. But it is not only that my own living longer is a large intrinsic good or satisfaction to me, and that therefore I greatly value the means to the end.

Here is another fact. Someone else's living longer may be the same to me. It may even be more to me. It is our ordinary nature to want our children to live longer, and of course to want them to have the means to that end. Do I not know a lot of people who give up a lot in their lives for their children, perhaps for their long-term lovers? To stick to exactly the subject, do I not know a lot of people who would secure more living-time for their children at the cost of shorter lives for themselves? They want more of existence for their children more than they want more of it for themselves. You can think this is something to give us some pride in humankind.

Are there counter-examples to these propositions about the great good of living longer? The killers who flew the airliners into the Twin Towers may come to mind. They chose not only to destroy the lives of so many others, but also to shorten their own. They did the medievally awful thing that they did, we are told, in religious confidence of a life to come, in confidence of immortality. If that is really true, whatever else is to be said of them, they of course were choosing *not* to shorten their existence, but rather to prolong it indefinitely. Their terrible acts, whatever else is to be said of them, do not count against the proposition that living longer is a great good to which we want the means.

Shall we think instead, as I am at least half-inclined to, that the killers of September 11 were not likely to have been certain in an ordinary sense of having lives after death? That they were not likely to have had a literal belief in a personal life after death? Such a literal belief is not common, even among the religious. Asserting such a belief it is perhaps as likely to be a matter of hope, or of stiffening one's resolve, or of moral and political self-proclamation. But put September 11 aside for a while.

It certainly is a fact that some men and women throughout history have given up their lives for a great or anyway a necessary cause, the cause of their people, a cause that we can take to have been great or necessary. Many hunger strikers have carried on to the end, and at least some of them did so without any belief in immortality. This fact goes together with more ordinary but relevant facts of serious risk-taking, say in war or in the protection of others in accidents or in rescue attempts. Some of us *do* sacrifice our lives. Captain Oates walked out into Antarctica saying he would be gone for some time.

Come to think of it, I daresay quite a few Americans, and not all of them related to the victims, would have given up their lives, committed suicide, to prevent what happened at the Twin Towers. There isn't much doubt about that. There are ordinary suicides too, quite a lot of them.

All these facts need to be granted, but they are consistent with the truth that living longer, going on existing, is a great thing wanted for itself by almost all of us, and that we also want the means to it.

Other great goods

There is a second truth, of the same size. It is that living longer is not only an end or intrinsic good, and a great good, but also itself a means to other things – to things that make for a good life. Certainly we do not only want to live longer. A good life is also one that has in it what living longer gives us more of – well-being, happiness, fulfillment, contentment, or something on the way to these. A good life involves, more particularly, great goods in addition to living longer. For you, these are things possessed by yourself and those who are close to you. They are satisfactions different from the elementary one of existing. These too are intrinsic goods, whatever further use they also are.

One is a quality of life in something like the sense put aside in passing above. This is a general quality of life that can be secured by, and more or less defined by, the possession of familiar material means. It is physical well-being tied to certain material goods. Some of these means are nearly as old as our kind, say a private place to live, and more and different food than is necessary to sustain life. A place to sit, maybe a cushion. Something to drink other than water. Other things that make for a decent quality of life in this sense are means of alleviating pain, or some of it, and help in dealing with disability, and protection from common dangers, and maybe the means of travelling a bit. There are also the well-advertised means that now have the name of being consumer-goods. They can come to seem to be necessities. They are easier to be superior about if you have a lot of them.

In addition to this physical well-being based on certain material goods, there are four other great goods to which living longer is also a means – at any rate by my way of counting. One, whether or not more important than the others to follow, or more important than physical well-being, has to do with freedom and power of various kinds, to which can be added safety. There is also respect and self-respect, and private and public relationships with others, and the satisfactions of culture, including religion and diversion. This is one way of getting much of a good life into focus. More of these five great goods is better than fewer of them, and more of each one is better than less. That is so, at any rate, for the overwhelming majority of us who have not reached real satiety.

As you have heard, living longer is a means to these other parts of a good life, a necessary condition. It is necessary for you to live longer in order to have a goodly amount. That amount, I guess, is one familiar in a kind of life known to me and many others, in apartments and houses in places like London, New Haven, Brooklyn, Toronto and Somerset. You can end up with a swimming pool.

So much for the great good that is living longer oneself, and one's family or close person also living longer, say to about seventy-five. So much too for this being a means to the other great goods. So much for those other goods themselves, beginning with physical well-being tied to having certain material things. Let us now look at the extent to which these human desires are realized, some details, both in the apartments and houses we know about and also elsewhere.

Half-lives and under-fives

Some people, because of their societies, have average lifetimes of about seventy-eight years. Some other people, because of their different societies, live on average about forty years. That is to say that the first group have lives of very different lengths, of which the average is about seventy-eight years. Some individuals bring the average up, some bring it down. So with the second group – they have different lengths of life, averaging about forty years.

It is of course necessary not to drift towards thinking instead of two groups of people, one with all its members dying at seventy-eight and one with all its members dying at forty. The two groups defined by the averages can have in them people dying at every age. What it comes to, you can say, is that fewer members of the second group get through each stage of life, say boyhood, young womanhood, parenthood, working life, early retirement.

What the thing comes to, you can also say, more to the point, is that many people in the second group, those people who pull its average down to forty rather than lift it up to that, have *half-lives at best*. That is a proper summary of their difference from the first group.

The distance between the two averages is great, and conveys a great deal about living-time. The average lifetimes of seventy-eight and forty could suggest to someone overhearing this talk of lifetimes, but not knowing exactly our subject, that we are concerned with two different species. The elephant and the horse, if you know about that sort of thing. The numbers of people involved are also very large. About 44 million in the unlucky group that includes half-lives. About 736 million in the first group.

The first group are in fact the populations of the United States, Canada, the United Kingdom, France, Germany, Italy, Spain, Denmark and Japan. The second group are the populations of the African countries of Malawi, Mozambique, Zambia and Sierra Leone.

A certain statistic about a first stage of life is sometimes given attention. It is taken to be a large or very significant part of the explanation of the averages of seventy-eight and forty years for the two groups. Sometimes it is taken to be more of the explanation than it is. In any case, you may think this fact is of significance for itself. It is a difference having to do with children.

With respect to the first group of people, the Americans and the rest of us, the number of children who die under the age of five, for each 1,000 live births, is only about *five or six*. Another good thing in itself, you may come to say. With respect to the second group of people, those in Malawi, Mozambique, Zambia, and Sierra Leone, things are different. Have a look at the table of figures. For every 1,000 children born alive, about *200* die under the age of five. A dark fact. An evil, to make less contentious use of a term than some do.

Necessary inquiry

The dark fact and the half-lives should move you, and so it is not too soon, reader, to say what is being asked of you now. Whatever our eventual conclusions, it is not that you should already be contemplating certain judgements having to do with the dying children and the low average lifetimes. You are not being prompted or elbowed towards moral judgements, thoughts of moral rights and obligations, let alone moralizing, having to do with these innocent persons.

That is, whatever our eventual conclusions, you are not being prompted by me to be on the way to judging seemingly relevant actions – actions, practices, ways of running things, policies and institutions of those of us in the first group as against the second. You are not being asked to judge that what we and our governments and corporations have done or not done with respect to the short lifetimes and the dying children is *wrong* – that our actions and the like ought to have been different, that we could reasonably expect bad effects.

Nor are you asked to make connected but different judgements, not on exactly our actions and the like but on us. One of these would take us as *responsible* for the dying children and the short lifetimes. That is, it would take us to be causes of those facts – trace them back at least partly to us, regard us as human causes of them.

There is an ambiguity there that is worth getting into focus in anticipation of things to come. You can take someone as responsible

country	average lifetimes in years	average healthy lifetimes in years	children dying under 5, per 1000 live births	rich/poor country: GNP per person in US dollars	worst-off 10th of population: % of total income or consumption	best-off 10th of population: % of total income or consumption
USA	77	70.0	7	29,240	1.8	30.5
Canada	79	72.0	6	19,170	2.8	23.8
UK	77	71.7	6	21,410	2.6	27.3
France	78	73.1	5	24,210	2.8	25.1
Germany	77	70.4	5	26,570	3.3	23.7
Italy	78	72.7	6	20,090	3.5	21.8
Spain	78	72.8	6	14,100	2.8	25.2
Denmark	76	69.4	5	33,040	3.6	20.5
Japan	80	74.5	4	32,350	4.8	21.7
Malawi	39	29.4	213	210	?	?
Mozambique	44	34.4	206	210	2.5	31.7
Zambia	40	30.3	202	330	1.6	39.2
Sierra Leone	38	25.9	316	140	0.5	43.6
Afghanistan	46*	37.7*	257*	?	?	?
Turkmenistan	67	54.3	74	370	2.6	31.7
Pakistan	64	55.9	136	470	4.1	27.6
Iraq	63	55.3	125	?	?	?
Iran	69	60.5	33	1,650	?	?
Saudi Arabia	72	64.5	26	6,910	?	?
United Arab Emirates	75	65.4	10	18,870	?	?
Israel	78	70.4	6	16,180	2.8	26.9
Palestine	71	?	?	3,097	?	?
India	63	53.2	105	440	3.5	33.5
Russia	67	61.3	25	2,260	1.7	38.7
Poland	73	66.2	11	3,910	3.0	26.3
China	70	62.3	47	750	2.4	30.4
Cuba	76	68.4	8	?	?	?
Libya	70	59.3	24	?	?	?
Brazil	67	59.1	42	4,630	0.9	47.6
Mexico	72	65.0	35	3,840	1.4	42.8
Argentina	73	66.7	22	8,030	?	?
Australia	78	73.2	5	20,640	2.0	25.4

The figures in columns 2, 4, 5, 6, and 7 come from *The World Guide 2001–2002*, pp. 24–5 and 602–9, and were derived from the World Bank's *World Development Indicators 2000*, The World Bank; *The State of the World's Children*, UNICEF 2000. The third column comes from The World Health Organization's *Healthy Life Expectancy Rankings*. To calculate a healthy life figure, years of ill-health are weighted as to severity and subtracted from the overall life expectancy.

Note that the fifth column is about GNP per person and the sixth and seventh about shares of total income or consumption. It would have been better to have had dollar figures for total income or consumption, but the two sets of statistics do certainly allow for the comparisons and absolute judgements made. GNP is the value of the total production of goods and services by an economy within national borders, plus income from abroad and minus income in the economy that goes abroad.

* All the figures in the table derive from 1994–8 data. In particular, the figures for Afghan average lifetimes, average healthy lifetimes and children dying under 5 derive from 1998 data, i.e. before the attack by the West.

---

for something before you have any idea as to the goodness or badness of the thing – all you believe is that it was owed to him and his intention. But you can also take someone as responsible for an action or its effect and mean not only that they intentionally initiated it. You also mean either that it was a bad thing and they are therefore to be disapproved of for it or worse, or it was a good thing and they are to be approved of for it – that is, they are to be held responsible or credited with responsibility. As a result of these attitudes, they may be blamed, condemned or punished, or praised or rewarded.

As I say, it is too soon to be judging actions or judging persons for them with respect to the dying children and the short lives. It is also too soon for another sort of thing that moral philosophers have distinguished, often speaking here of *the good man*, to which we now must add the good woman. This is judging us not with respect to particular actions, practices and so on, but judging our general worth as persons, our general moral standing. You are not asked to judge that our whole lives and natures, to which all our actions and activities are relevant, have been selfish and low or human or decent or whatever.

It may be, for all I intend to convey by the figures, that all our lives in both groups are as they have to be. In particular, that we and our politicians and boards of directors and international finance couldn't be or do otherwise. That it actually is true, as the seventeenth-century philosopher and metaphysician Leibniz bravely supposed, that of all the possible worlds that there might have been, this is the best one – our world is the best possible world. That the many shorter lives are not the avoidable little upshots of our chosen foreign policies and our economic organizing. There is a long tradition of political thought, incidentally, a kind of conservatism, that includes and rests on just those thoughts.

This book is an inquiry in which you are asked to participate. It is an inquiry into terrorism and ourselves, although one brought on by the shock of September 11, 2001, when all with television sets were present for the killing. An evil of another kind – some say moral rather than natural. An inquiry, also, into the aftershocks of September 11. One was that the thing seen on the screen was possible, the medieval horror without any of the respectability we attach to our wars, or our side in our wars. Also, even more of the same was possible, since some restraining god was dead.

Another aftershock was hearing what was said quietly around the world, and despite the horror and the automatism of our leaders. It was said, not just in cosmopolitan London but in Somerset too, that the Americans had it coming, that they were being given some of their own back. They would have to learn and change, grow up. It was said that it was the treatment of the Palestinians by the Jews in Palestine and also the ones in New York and Washington that was the cause. It would have been better to mention more of us than just Americans and Jews.

Inquiry is needed, moral inquiry, near to moral philosophy. This is not the only kind of slow and careful thinking about terrorism that is needed. Such books of relevant politics and economics are needed, and of the records of governments, and of history and international relations, and such books by good journalists. But arguably general moral inquiry is the main kind of inquiry that is needed, anyway one main kind. Other kinds lead towards it, or presuppose it, or bluff about it, or take it to be easy, or try to do it on the wing.

It is true on this day, as these words are written, that the ending of this book is unknown to me. Something has happened to us that calls for new reflection on the decency and indecency of human lives, ours as well as theirs, and makes it harder. This doubt is not just a minority's. It cannot be concealed by our brave leaders in their seeming single-mindedness and uprightness and our kinds and degrees of compliance with them. It lingers in their sentences and in our newspapers and on our screens, in and between and under the lines. It is still the state of mind, as it seems to me, of most of us who were present for the killing at the Twin Towers and have followed what has come after.

Let us make our inquiry as real as we can. As I say, let us not rush to take any of us in the well-heeled world as having done wrong with respect to the low average lifetimes and the dying children, been responsible, been inhuman in our lives. There *are* great tragedies that at least seem to be without wrong actions, culpably responsible agents, bad or awful characters. Some are the natural disasters, say floods and fires. They are things of which all of us know, nonetheless, that it is bad or worse that they happen.

It *is* bad in this way that many people live less long than they could, that so many of their children die. These, to say the least, are bad lives. There is no point in trying to put aside feeling about that. We are not the one or two dessicated calculating machines that the feelingful Aneurin Bevan thought he noticed among his fellow members in England's old Labour Party back in about 1950. That was the one, by the way, that founded the National Health Service, because it could do more than count. Still, our object now is to get a grip on facts of several kinds, for the first time in the case of some of us, once again in the case of others. The facts must be all the relevant facts. Of necessity, then, they must include what is said by those who are against us.

But one more word first on the nature of this moral inquiry. It was indeed brought on by feelings about September 11 and the days afterward in Afghanistan. But it will be more general than other investigations, as philosophy and near-philosophy by their nature are. It will not get nearly so far into history, politics and economics as other investigations – not so far into propositions taken by some of us as being of deniable kinds. It can have its essential basis, if certainly not its only basis, in well-established general facts, those in the table above.

It will also be more general not only in considering general moralities and in spending some time on the general definition of terrorism and on other large things, but also in having to do not only with actual terrorism but also with some possible and some conceivable terrorism against us – and of course having to do with us, things we can learn about ourselves. You can find out about yourself not only from what people do to you, but also from what somebody might have the idea of doing to you, with some kind of reason, whether or not they bring themselves to do it.

To think of some different terrorism, and different judgements about us it may bring to mind, is not just to have the recommendation of a broader view. It is, for a start, to have something of more practical use, about the possible future, not just the past. You can't be sure about the future. As we know, it can be a lot different from the past. There is also another recommendation of generality. It will tell us more about precisely September 11 and what followed it, by putting this in a context or range of comparisons. Also, in the same way, the generality will tell us more about precisely our own moral situation with respect to September 11. You do not know a thing's nature without having a grip on similar, related and different things.

The general and larger aim of this moral inquiry of ours, with its particular recommendations, is another reason for not rushing.

Less than half-lives, and a reason

To the figures so far given can be added some related ones that tell more of the same story. They have to do with years of life that are *not healthy* – calculated years resulting from counting or weighing actual years differently on account of more or less serious malady or disability. Someone's healthy years of life so conceived, then, may be fewer than their actual years of life. The number of healthy years is the result of cancer, heart disease, mental illness, emaciation by hunger, AIDs, river blindness, malaria and so on. It may also be the result of ten or twenty years of civil war, whatever the war's immediate and earlier causes.

The average healthy lifetime of our group, the one with the United States in it, is about seventy-two years. The average healthy lifetime of the other group, with Malawi in it, is about thirty years. At each stage of life, so many fewer in that group were healthy, so many more of them sick or worse. To go back to ordinary life-expectancies, as you heard, many in the African countries in question have half-lives at best. They are the individuals who bring the average down. In terms of healthy life – *decent life* – many have *less than half-lives at best*. Some of these lives that bring the average years down to thirty must be lives that we for our part would be inclined to take as not worth living.

You will have noticed that most of the countries of the world have been left out of the story here and earlier, the chosen groups. There are countries that come close enough in the rankings to those of the first group, say Australia, Ireland and Portugal. So too are there countries fairly close to the African group, say Chad. What has been and will be said about the chosen two groups of countries applies with amendment to some others. It seems to me a good idea, in order to have things clearer, to focus more closely to start with – on us in the United States and so on and on to the African group at the other end of the scale. But we and they are not all of the story. No one in Chad will think so.

Let us go on. It was said at the beginning that it is because of their societies that people in the two groups have the average lifetimes they do. I had in mind that the immediate or proximate cause was the state of each society, whatever causes further back there may be of that immediate or proximate cause. It has sometimes been half-supposed that short lives are all about climate or race or something as natural. It has sometimes been forgotten that money can buy ways of dealing with heat and even with the destroyer AIDs. That is true of famine or starvation too.

No one half-informed and in a state of calm will be surprised at a connection between general conditions of wealth and poverty, the things you can buy with what money you have, and the differences so far glanced at in average lengths of life and in childhood mortality. Still, to make any judgements, we need more than an impression of what gives rise to the lifetimes we have been contemplating – the half-lives, those of the dying children and their parents, those of the sick.

The United States, however it shares out its money among its citizens, of which you will hear something in a moment, has had $29,240 per citizen each year. Sierra Leone, translating into the same currency, has had $140. The average for the whole group with the United States in it is about *$24,000* a year. The average for the African group is about *$220* a year. The cost of a special lunch for me and my publisher. The people to think of first, again, are those who bring the annual average down to $220.

There is an immense difference, then, in means to well-being, a difference that explains half-lives, dying children, sick lives.

Reassuring ourselves

There is something else that has to do with wealth or poverty. In a way, you may say, it can give us a better conscience. The United States comes at the head of a list again, in this case the mentioned wealthy countries listed in terms of the distribution of things *within* each of them. The worst-off tenth of Americans has had 1.8 per cent of the country's total income or consumption. Not a lot. The richest tenth of the population has had 30.5 per cent. The sharing-out in the other wealthy countries is similar. But to turn to the African group, the figures for the bottom and the top tenths in Sierra Leone are 0.5 per cent and 43.6 per cent. The inequalities in this group are a little greater than the inequalities in ours.

You may therefore note that Sierra Leone, to the extent that it makes sense to speak of it as an entity after prolonged civil war, is not doing well for the bottom tenth of its own people. If the World Bank has something to do with its state, so does its capital of Free-town or maybe its generals. So with the other African countries. There may be an occasion later for the thought that the conditions of social altruism, according to the figures, are a little better in Canada

– that the African countries are not so concerned with their own impoverished as they might be. This may also be the occasion for the thought that all of us under the sun, all humankind, Canada or Sierra Leone, have something in common.

If you are uneasily preparing yourself for moral argument, preparing to defend yourself against what may be coming, another contrast can be noticed by you. We have it so far that the four African countries have average lifetimes of about forty years, and related average healthy lifetimes, and deaths of children at the rate of 200 per every 1,000 children born, and are so poor as to have an average of merely about $220 per person a year as against $24,000 for us.

The situation of the four African countries is therefore worse than that of a group of Islamic countries save for Afghanistan – Afghanistan before the war on the Taliban and Osama bin Laden and his followers by the United States and its allies. For these Islamic countries of Turkmenistan, Pakistan, Iraq, Iran, Saudi Arabia and the United Arab Emirates, the average lifetime is about sixty-eight years. The deaths of children before five are about sixty-seven per 1,000. The income or consumption is an average of something over $4,000.

So if anyone should wish to throw a tolerant light on terrorism by citing lifetime-related facts, and in particular a tolerant light on Islamic terrorism, can they not rightly be given pause by the *African* facts and the absence of *African* terrorists? Can they not have it conveyed to them that it seems not to be actual deprivation or suffering that gives rise to killing, but something else less understandable, less easy to sympathize with? Religion in at least its outward form? Pride? Racial pride? The kind of pride that allows Lebanese businessmen to mistreat their black servant girls from Sierra Leone?

Another contrast, another possibility of reassurance for us, is akin to what was remarked a moment ago about the best-off tenths within the African populations and their very limited altruism with respect to their less fortunate fellows in the worst-off tenths. Things are in a way similar in the Islamic world. The circumstances of Saudi Arabia and the United Arab Emirates are significantly different from those of the other Islamic countries, say Pakistan and Turkmenistan.

See the figures. The two oil-rich states seem not to be doing a great deal to alleviate the harder conditions of life among other Muslims.

Quarter-lives

But let us return to brute facts about lifetimes, some different ones. They have a different tendency, the same as before, not reassuring.

In the United States or Britain or Spain or Japan, does the financially best-off tenth of population live longer than any other tenth? The American and British figures for these tenths of population seem not to be collected, anyway according to the governmental statistics people. But there can be no doubt, whatever little qualifications there are of the fact, that the best-off tenth in our group of countries does live longer than most of the other tenths and of course the bottom one. It has more children making it through to the age of five too.

We will be noticing some nearby national statistics later about blacks and whites and social classes (p. 116) that confirm the fact about the best-off tenth, but we all know without the aid of statistics about the connection between really good medical attention, to say nothing of food, and living longer. We know about poverty and poor health too. There are many other relevant facts, including the large one noticed a little way back, that people in general live a lot longer in well-off countries than in poor ones.

So if the average life expectancy for one of our countries as a whole is about seventy-eight years, what is the average life expectancy of the *best-off* tenth?

The same question arises about a lot of other people – the *bottom* tenth of people in Malawi, Mozambique, Zambia and Sierra Leone. If the average lifetimes for all taken together in those places are about forty, how long do the bottom tenth live?

Well, I have to leave you to find your own answers, not easy to come by, or to speculate with me. Is it not very probable that the top tenth in the United States and like places lives for about eighty years on average? Almost certainly. Do the bottom tenth in Sierra Leone and the like places have average lifetimes of about thirty years? On the basis of the very great inequality of income or consumption between bottom and top tenths – 0.5 per cent and 43.6 per cent – and various other comparisons and considerations, some mentioned above in connection with the United States or the like, it is a safe conjecture, to my mind a certainty.

It was noted at the start, about the two groups of societies taken as wholes, that the average lifetimes of seventy-eight and forty years meant that many people in the second group, those that bring its average down, have half-lives at best. In terms of healthy years, many had considerably less than half-lives at best. What is to be said about our comparison now, between the best-off tenth among us and the worst-off tenth among them? One thing is that many people in the latter tenth, those that pull its average down to thirty, have *quarter-lives at best*, somewhere around twenty years.

It is easily said. But the disparity in living-time between these two well-defined sets of human beings is not something we see clearly. We are not faced with it. We do not see it as we saw the awful killing at the Twin Towers. By way of our screens, we were there, and we brought our own experience and knowledge with us. It was people like us on the planes. Seeing an emaciated child on television is not the same. Another world. We will come back to the subject, or near to it. But it is useful to keep in mind now, about those four million whose lives averaged thirty years, and those among them with the quarter-lives at best, that each of them had a name, and hopes.

Is there a reason, from the point of view of moral inquiry, to restrain my own feelings in what follows? Well, it is not as if openness about them will deprive you of yours. Nor must the best policy always be what seems to be moderation, or even what really is moderation. Also, some openness will let you know the nature of your guide. More books should be explicit about their authors, as more politicians, notably more American politicians, should be explicit about their mixed allegiances, obligations or calculations.

And, finally, actual attitudes, as distinct from what can seem to be said for or against them at first, are as proper a part of an inquiry at the beginning as at any other time. Somebody's firmness of feeling on a subject can give rise to more reflection on the part of somebody else. It will do no harm to your understanding, either, to reflect that some feelings you encounter in these pages may be had by very many more people than your own.

Larger numbers

A final reflection about living-time may not be popular. It may strike some as contentious, distasteful or worse. Contentious, they will say, because what it comes to is somewhat unclear. Distasteful because it may be taken to imply an equivalence between dyings and killings. Something will be said of that too, when we are more concerned with interpretations of facts. For the moment, remember that popularity is not the aim of an inquiry worth the name, as it is not the aim of a court worth the name.

The worst-off tenth of population in the four African countries, to repeat, have average lifetimes of about thirty years. Thus they live for an average of something like fifty years less than the average of the best-off tenth in the wealthy countries. The exact facts do not matter for a certain question. If things had been different for a good while, would they have lived as long as the best-off tenth in those very different places? Or something like that?

Suppose we in the United States, the United Kingdom and so on had put in something equivalent to a war-effort on their behalf, or just really worked at it. The Prime Minister Mr Blair in one or two of his speeches might have been taken almost to be speaking of doing such a thing sometime in the future. People were moved. If we had really worked at it, would the worst-off tenth have gained fifty years of life on average?

Do you say instead, for whatever reason, perhaps a superiority to utopian speculation, that the best that could have been done by our human exertions to improve the conditions of the worst-off tenth would have resulted in their gaining only thirty years of living-time on average? Or do you say, out of more caution, or an assumption about our common human nature or whatever, that even if we had tried, the African tenths would have gained only fifteen years on average? Or only ten? Or only five?

Good lives, bad lives

Do you say that it is irrelevant that between 1920 and 1940, American whites came to live longer lives by about ten years? And in the next two decades by another six years? And between 1960 and 1980 by about four years, and between 1980 and 1998 by another three years?

It actually does not matter a lot to the argument whether you say the African tenth could have gained fifty years of life on average or only five. In the African tenth of population, you need to remember, there are over four million people. It does not matter a lot to the argument how few more years of life they would have had on average if we had tried. The loss of living-time because we did not try is still immense. To shorten lives or leave lives short is not the same as to kill. It is not like killing. We know that before we begin to think more about it. It is still true that the living-time lost to the innocent people under consideration is such as to make all deaths by terrorism, considered only in terms of living-time lost, insignificant. This is not a congenial idea, but it is an idea that some parties to a real inquiry will take to be relevant. They may take it to be more relevant than anything else. They will say they are not flies.

They will say it too when someone on their side gets more particular and argues, rightly, that there is solid evidence to show we could have lengthened the lives in question by just five years – and draws the conclusion that there was a loss of living-time of *20 million years*. Do you say that this is unreal? Crazy stuff? It would be good to know what you mean. Certainly the conclusion is hard to face. But how could it be mistaken to think of it?

They will also say they are not flies when they remind us that we are dealing with a sample, only a bottom tenth of population of four countries. They will say they are not flies when someone proposes going on to other simple calculations, including one having to do with the figure mentioned at the start, that forty years is the average lifetime for the entire populations of the four African countries. They may say that the main thing about killing *is* the shortening of life, and that there is something akin to intentionality on our part, anyway akin to responsibility, in the loss of living-time in the African countries.

We will be looking at that large matter in due course. But now let us turn from this first part of a good life if you have one – living long enough – to the second part. This, as remarked earlier, has to do with what can be given the name of well-being and can be conceived in terms of the satisfactions of the five great desires other than the desire for a decent length of life. These are for a quality of life resting on and defined by certain material goods, and for freedom and power, respect and self-respect, relationships both private and public, and the satisfactions of a culture.

Great goods again

All this can be put differently, in terms of what have already been in view, and can again mildly be called *bad lives*. You can have a life that is bad because it is short – a half-life or a quarter-life. This has been our concern so far. But you can have a life that is bad not because it is short but because of other facts – your being deprived of some or all of the other great goods just mentioned. Reflection on the exact definition of a bad life will come later (p. 53). Our present subject is to get some kind of knowledge of lives that are recognizably bad for reasons other than shortness.

We have a start on this subject in the short lives. It is not only that living longer is a necessary means to other parts of a good life. Living longer is also something different, a pretty good indicator of having the five other things or anyway some of them. A short life is a pretty good indicator of not having the five other things or all of them, first of all a quality of life connected with certain material goods. But we can come to see more than this grim generalization about some of the bad lives in question.

To glance again across the table, the differences in the figures between the second and third columns, about lifetimes and healthy lifetimes, give you the average years of bad health for a country. In terms of Zambia, the average years of bad health are about ten. If you are a Zambian man or woman who pulls the average down to ten – perhaps someone with twenty years of severe debility – the question barely arises of your doing tolerably in your life in terms of the mentioned great goods. You will do badly, of course, in terms of quality of life having to do with certain material goods, since they include medical means you lack. You will not have much energy to indulge in self-respect either, or in relationships with a chosen person or a wider community.

Still thinking of relationships, there is another kind of hurt that comes to mind in connection with the dying children in the fourth column – the hurt, say, of a mother in Malawi that helps to bring the number of children dying under five up to an average of 213 for every 1,000 live births. I suppose the human experience of seeing your four-year-old die is different if a lot of four-year-olds are dying? Or if a child of yours has died before, maybe two? Is the experience of seeing your four-year-old die very much different? There is one more question, though. Is it proper for us, in our thinking, to take the difference into account?

As we know, there is a strong connection between income or consumption and the great goods that are our subject now. You cannot live as a scavenger on a refuse dump outside a South American capital and have any of these great goods. Very likely the same is to be said of all of the bottom tenths in Brazil and Mexico, who have only 0.9 per cent and 1.4 per cent of the total income or consumption of the countries. Certainly the great goods are not had by the many individuals who bring the averages down to 0.9 and 1.4 per cent. As against what the best-off tenths get of what is going, which is 47.6 per cent and 42.8 per cent.

Things are worse with respect to great goods for the worst-off tenths in the Islamic countries, perhaps including the oil states who keep their figures to themselves. They are still worse for the bottom tenths in the African countries. If, as in Zambia, the average share of GNP is $330 and the bottom tenth has 1.6 per cent of income and consumption, then the bottom tenth has no goods worth mentioning in terms of well-being.

Despite cultural differences and lower expectations, there is a true proposition that they want the kinds of things we want. They have hardly anything. A detail may be useful. It is that the only easy place they have to defecate in may pollute the only water they have to drink. Do you say that surely they could walk further? That they are ignorant? Yes, they are ignorant. Did they need to be ignorant? Did God arrange that?

Other hopeful remarks can be made, some by economists. Will someone remark that the equivalent of a dollar goes further in Zambia than it does in Canada? True enough, but not so true as to take the sharp edges off the things we have been contemplating. Will someone say that some of the poor are happier than some of the rich? No doubt. I myself am among the rich, by a reasonable definition, and not quite so happy as a dancing lad I can imagine with nothing much, maybe a dancing Afghan lad with a kite.

But will the happy poor not be a small fraction of those mothers, say, whose children are very thin, like the ones in the Oxfam photos? Will the happy poor be numerous among those people who know the stigma that they are under, their being beneath the awareness of the people in the cars? Will there be many happy poor among those who especially would like to be able to read the printed words they look at every day? Or among those dying with AIDS?

More reassurance?

Some last reflections on the table. It is true that several of the best-off tenths have extraordinary shares of what is available in their societies – look at Brazil and Mexico, and also Sierra Leone. Still, there is a considerable likeness between all the listed countries in this respect – all the groups in the table, us and all of them. Each of the best-off tenths has very roughly 30 per cent of what there is, and each of the worst-off tenths has something like 2 per cent or 3 per cent.

It would be misleading to use these figures casually with the matter of physical well-being tied to certain material goods. This is so since the worst-off tenth in Australia, say, has 2 per cent or 3 per cent of a large total for the society, and the worst-off tenth in Mozambique has that share of a very small total. But think instead of the good of freedom and power, and the good of respect and self-respect. These are by their nature *relative* goods – how much I have of freedom in our society depends on how much you have. So too, roughly, with respect and self-respect.

Could this turn out to be a source of comfort to us? Shall we be able to say that there is a good reason for supposing that the very poor in the four African countries and others are no more short on freedom and power within their societies, and also on respect and self-respect, than the very poor in the United States and the like? It is worth thinking about. So is something else.

As remarked, all of the best-off tenths in all the countries in the table – those where the figures are available and published – have very roughly about 30 per cent of what is going. This is as true of the four African countries and some of the Islamic countries as it is of our own group of countries with the United States at its head. It is true of the three South American countries, and India and Australia, and also the ex-Communist states of Russia, Poland and China. Is this a law of nature, anyway a law of human nature? Is it something that it is or would be futile to protest about or fight against?

What would this law of human nature come to? Well, all of the best-off tenths, wherever they are, have a lot in common and also, you might think, a common interest. Such a common interest is different from the common interest of each best-off tenth with the rest of the people of its own country. Take the interest of a Mexican executive of a transnational corporation setting up a further low-wage assembly plant in Mexico across the border from America. Is his interest not an interest that conflicts with the interests of the Mexican women in the plant? And coincides with the interest of his American colleagues?

So is the law of nature just an ordinary fact? Is it the ordinary fact, about which something might be done, that people make profitable agreements that have a dark side? You do not need an ideology in order to come to a tentative answer.

It is clear, anyway, that the inequalities in the table are not all between whole populations or groups of whole populations. Not all disparities are between us, all of us, in the United States, the United Kingdom and so on, and all of them in the four African countries or the Islamic countries. Some inequalities are between (1) just some of us in each of the fortunate countries together with just some of them in the African and Islamic countries on the one hand, and, on the other hand, (2) others of us in the fortunate countries and others of them in the African and Islamic countries. Natural alliances, not limited to only the very top tenths, could enter into explanations of the fact of very many bad lives.

Like it or not, an inquiry into us with respect to terrorism will have to be an inquiry especially into some of us, won't it? Maybe including me, and you.

Not an omission

All of what has been noticed so far, about lives that are bad because they are short, and lives that are bad because of deprivation, and of course lives that are bad for both reasons, raises a question about us and some of us especially and the leaders we have. The question comes up even if we take things slowly. It has to do with the rightness of our not changing things, leaving the world as it is. It has to do, that is, largely or anyway primarily, with the rightness of what are called our *omissions* – and with our responsibility in them and the decency of our lives.

But it is not only a question of our omissions that is raised by our critics. Our critics say more, that we do not merely leave things wrong, but also put them wrong. They say positive actions of ours, our commissions, are as relevant to bad lives as our omissions. They make particular accusations about our positive actions and so on, past and present. There are positive actions of the United States with respect to South America, into which it has intruded many times. A good record has been kept by able judges. There are positive actions of Britain with respect to colonies and ex-colonies. There are also the actions of our transnational corporations, now as important in some ways as our governments and administrations.

As remarked earlier (p. 11) our inquiry will have its essential basis in certain well-established general facts, those in the table. They bring to mind our possible omissions before our positive actions. But, as remarked earlier, and as just noticed again, our inquiry will also need to give some attention to another possible basis for judgement – our positive actions. These, the main or only concern of other strong lines of inquiry, have to be kept in mind. If we do not have to take up this agenda of our critics, we cannot ignore it.

Let us attend to it a little. It would be at least difficult, and probably not enlightening, to try to proceed in a general way about our commissions. The charges against us are more particular than in the case of our omissions. Instead of trying to assemble a table of figures, it will be better to look at a particular case. There is the additional reason that it has been taken, wrongly or rightly, as the outstanding cause of the terrorism that seized our concentration on September 11 and subsequently gave rise to our counter-attack on Islamic terror. The case is that of Palestine, and thus of Israel and the United States.

Here it will not be possible to avoid moving closer to moral judgement on groups and individuals and on their acts. Still, our business now is mainly or in the first instance factual. As for the facts, there is more room for mistake and self-deception here than in this inquiry up until now. I shall take care to limit myself to propositions that seem to me more or less indisputable. As for the choice of propositions, choosing what to leave out, this cannot be easy. Still, you can try to put in what each side takes to be of greatest relevance. Despite the chance of mistake and self-deception, impartiality and independence of mind are possible. It is usually a piece of strategy on one side or the other to deny this.

The land of Palestine, despite the contribution of the Bible to misconceptions, apparently was a land of Semites in the beginning – Semites being speakers of a certain family of languages – and except for a longer and a shorter interlude, brief in terms of its long history, it remained such a land until very recently. That is, it was settled around 4,000 BC and remained Semitic rather than Hebrew in particular except for a few centuries around 700 BC and a shorter time around the birth of Christ. It was such despite Egyptian, Roman and other empires having sway over it. It was consecrated for Judaism and Christianity, so to speak, by the history of the Old Testament and the birth and death of Christ. It was consecrated for Islam by Muhammad's veneration of it as a result of his embracing of the other two religions in his own.

What is the relevance of this ancient past? Are we conceivably to decide great matters of living-space and homelands now by ancient religion and its myths? Shall we start up all the world again by studying holy books? Do right and wrong now depend at all on what happened back then? Morality is about the living and those to come, isn't it? Is the remote past what the living really care about? They may say so, but is it really?

In 1900 there were 500,000 Arabs and 50,000 Jews in Palestine. Many of the latter had arrived as a result of the Zionist struggle for a homeland begun shortly before. This movement was the result of anti-Semitism, hostility to and prejudice against Jews, a unique history of contempt, envy, and persecution. The culture of the Arabs in 1900, judged from a Western point of view, was rudimentary. So too was their commercial activity. They could be and were spoken of as peasants. Their traditions of governing or social cooperation did not amount to a modern state. In 1917 Britain's foreign minister, Arthur Balfour, declared support for a national homeland for the Jews in Palestine, without prejudice to the rights of the overwhelmingly larger non-Jewish population. Arab opposition to further immigration into their homeland, including violence and a general strike in 1936, was disregarded. What is the relevance of this closer past?

The destruction of European Jews by Hitler and the Germans during the Second World War did not issue, as in justice it ought to have, in a Jewish state carved out of Germany. It eventually issued, rather, in the United Nations resolving on a certain partition of Palestine. There were 749,000 Arabs and 9,250 Jews in what would become the Arab state if the partition went ahead. There were 497,000 Arabs and 498,000 Jews in what would be the Jewish state.*

What happened instead of the agreed partition was partly the result of actions by Jewish terrorists, partly the result of international politics and familiarity with it, partly of sympathy, and partly of finance mainly from American and other Jews. What happened was Israel's humanly understandable proclamation of itself as an independent country in 1948, and its prompt recognition as such by us.

---

* These figures, like others in these pages, come from the best of brief accounts known to me of Palestine and Israel, in *The World Guide, 2001/2002* (Oxford, New Internationalist Publications), an annual international survey of notable independence of mind.

This was followed by its use of force and of terrorism, including the massacre of an entire village, led by Manachem Begin, subsequently Prime Minister of Israel. In the ensuing 1948 war begun by Arab countries, in which they sought to reclaim the Arab land, Israel took more land, nearly half as much again as resolved by the United Nations. The Palestinians remained stateless.

In the six-day war of 1967, which followed actions by Arab terrorists, the Jewish state seized the whole of Palestine. It did so with the use of American arms, and has since depended on America. By this time more than half of the Palestinians had been driven out of their homes or abandoned them in fear. They went to refugee camps, pens where they remained. The United Nations resolution calling Israel to withdraw from the occupied territories was ignored, by way of the argument that it needed secure borders, and with the necessary compliance of the United States and other powers.

Following Israel's 'Operation Peace for Galilea' in 1982, which was an invasion of Lebanon, there were appalling massacres of Arab civilians in the refugee camps of Sabra and Shetilla. For this terrorism another subsequent Prime Minister of Israel, Ariel Sharon, was held personally responsible by an inquiry forced on the Israeli government and conducted by it. In 1987 persistent terrorism by Arabs against Israelis was begun, part of the *intifada* or uprising. With interludes of negotiation and hope, there has been small-scale conflict since between the Israeli army and Palestinian civilians and armed organizations. The casualties have been overwhelmingly on the Arab side. There was been protest by a number of Israelis against their country.

Except for one period, the building of settlements on Arab land in the occupied territories has continued, which policy has been officially condemned by the United Nations but not prevented. Between 250,000 and 400,000 Soviet Jews were resettled on Arab land between 1989 and 1991. A third of the Palestinians in the occupied territories now live in refugee camps. To the Jewish diaspora has been added a Palestinian diaspora. Of about seven million Palestinians, about half are now outside of Palestine.

Official aid from the United States to Israel from 1949 had reached

$40 billion in 1967, this being 21.5 per cent of all American foreign aid. By 1991, also according to American figures, the amount reached $53 billion. United Nations resolutions against Israel have come to nothing because of the American veto in the Security Council. The Palestinian resistance, by comparison, has had to rely not on tanks and planes but on stones and suicide bombers.

In the spring of 2002, as a result of provocation by Prime Minister Sharon and then renewed suicide killings by Palestinians, and with the terrorism of September 11 as a further cause or pretext, Israel again made use of its army and airforce. Tanks encircled villages, the leader of the Palestinians was humiliated, rockets and armoured bulldozers wrecked homes, Red Cross ambulances trying to get to wounded and dying Palestinians were stopped, bodies of victims were disposed of by those who killed them, uncounted by their own side. It horrified the world, save for many Americans left uninformed by their media.

This was said to be Israel's war on terrorism. Was it terrorism itself? Would calling it terrorism be loose talk? A kind of exaggeration? Emotional? Like the Palestinian diplomat's remembering the Holocaust on the television news and saying his people were now the Jews of the Jews? That question will have to wait a while.

History is a proof that peoples demand the freedom that is their running of their own lives in a place to which their history and culture attaches them. It is a freedom for which oppressed people have always fought. It is a freedom such that a threat against it in 1939 united almost all of us against Germany. It has been denied to the Palestinians. Their bitterness is owed not only to bare fact of the loss of their homeland, so to speak, but to their having had it taken from them.

Palestinians have been denied by their enemy exactly this moral right of a people secured and defended by that enemy for itself. No fear or half-fear or pretended fear on the part of the Israelis, let alone talk of terrorism against democracy, can touch the enormity of this moral inconsistency. The essential American part in it is not lessened by its having been played, by most non-Jewish Americans, in a kind of absent-mindedness, sometimes wilful.

The terrible inconsistency is plain to all who are unblinded, plain to very many Jews in and out of Israel. No hair-splitting will help. It is as plain to those of us who also see that it was a moral necessity after the Second World War that the Jews come to have a homeland, in Palestine if not elsewhere. Add in about the inconsistency, if you want, that it is not the first one in the existence of a people or a person. Say there are inconsistencies in my existence, and in yours, and on the Arab side. No doubt. But some consistencies matter more. To mention another one, being consistent about saving lives is different from being consistent about saving Jewish lives.

It is not only the freedom of a people that has been denied to the Palestinians. Another thing, which can indeed be distinguished, is respect and self-respect. Having been the principal victims of racism in history, Jews now seem to have learned from their abusers. Zionism as it is has rightly been condemned as racist by the United Nations, whatever further analysis of the fact is attempted. As for the material goods that serve to provide a quality of life, they are in short supply in a refugee camp. So too is the culture of a people. With respect to the good of human relationships, no more needs to be remarked on than large numbers of wrecked families. These things are insults, too, indeed injuries, to the rest of the Arab world.

The bottom fact of it all, if not the only fact, is that the lives of several million people have been made what we are calling bad by wrongful actions of people who suffered uniquely before them – and by actions of their supporters elsewhere, mainly in America. It is inconceivable that the experience of the Palestinians does not open questions about the ensuing terrible actions by them and on their behalf, and about what we are to think and do. As much as what we were thinking about before, lengths of lifetimes in different places, Palestine opens questions about right and wrong in general, about our responsibility for what has gone wrong, about what really can be said in condemnation of the terrorism of September 11, and about our own moral relationship to that day and afterwards and about what is to be done now.

2
Natural and other morality

Natural morality

Could there be good lives and bad lives in a world without morality? Certainly there could be long-enough lives, say seventy-five years, and other great goods. Long-enough lives and other great goods presumably could exist and be valued without any question arising of who in particular ought to have what, who has a moral right to keep or get what. If this is not the case in our world as it is, something of the sort is certainly possible or conceivable.

It is true that something good would be missing from a world without right and wrong actions and moral responsibility and moral standing in it – your satisfaction in being treated rightly by someone else, according to your lights, where your feeling is about their goodwill or good intentions rather than just about the beneficial effect. The badness to you of someone's knowingly or carelessly injuring or cheating you would also be missing.

Still, as we have done already, we can keep the question of what things are good and bad pretty much separate from the fact of our concern with the rightness of ourselves and others having them, which is a large natural fact of our existence, and our resulting moral principles and the like. The concern and then the principles are our subjects now. If a moral inquiry starts with particular facts, or some of them, as ours has, its other early business must be the natural fact and practice of morality, and the resulting moral principles and doctrines by which we seek to shape it further, these being the work of great and not so great philosophers and others.

An inquiry cannot leap or work its way straight-off to particular judgements. Compare a court of law. No court worth having proceeds towards verdicts in a case on the basis of the facts and a judge's reactions on Tuesday. A court has to hand the institution of the law and its principles – a general resource, guide and constraint entirely necessary to any arguable judgement. This is more than a matter of particular statutes, laws and precedents.

We need some counterpart of the law, whether or not we can also have a moral code or the like. This counterpart is one large thing I had in mind earlier in speaking of the new uncertainty caused by September 11 (p. 11). We need to try to arrive at something whose lack has been explicit or implicit in our newspapers and on our screens. This is an understanding of the nature of morality, and, if not a proven set of moral principles, then the guidance that can come from contemplating a spectrum or anyway a representative few of them.

Morality itself, the nature of the social thing we find ourselves in rather than the various contending principles and what-not in which philosophers and others take it to issue, is a large subject, rarely treated briskly. Much is said along the way. It sticks in my mind, alas, that it was once written of a work on ethics that 'Professor Kerner is not attracted to the shortest distance between two points'. If the subject of a society's morality and its principles is essential to us, let us not emulate him.

Much the same fact as that there are good things, including long lives, is that we have desires. This has as much claim as anything else to be fundamental to our human nature as we now have it. More particularly we have desires to have the great goods for ourselves and for those close to us. You want kinds of freedom for you and yours, in the street or a job or the world, and to stop other people from frustrating these desires. This truth has had almost as much elaboration as the subject of the nature of morality. Most recently it has issued in the confusion that our genes are selfish, which would be hard for them since they have no desires.

A second truth about us and our nature is that we are subject to consistency, in a way rational. This is not to make a very large claim. For example, it is not to claim that we always adopt effective and economical means to whatever ends we have, a practice sometimes taken as the fundamental kind of rationality. It will come up again. Rather, our being subject to consistency is here to be understood, at bottom, as the fact that we have reasons for what we believe, want, ask for, demand, and do.

It is part of our having reasons that we are in a certain minimal way consistent, and cannot escape this consistency. It is not something we aspire to, try to learn, or even do learn. What it amounts to is that if today's weather is a reason for not walking along the stream to Mells, then if the weather is just the same tomorrow, that too will be a reason for not walking along the stream to Mells.

More generally, we have reasons and they are general. We do not say or think that a truth about an action can be a reason for it or the rightness of it if a like truth about a like action is not a reason for that other action. None of this is to be taken to imply, of course, that reasons are always or often overwhelming, that they do not conflict, that they cannot be overborne by other reasons, and so on.

A third thing about us is a kind of addition to the first – which was that we very much want to have good and avoid bad things for ourselves and such other close persons as our children. The addition is that we also have some sympathy for others *not* close to us, in fact for people in general unless we have been caught up in some hostility or hatred. To wake up in Korea after the flight and see a child in danger of drowning or just falling down, in the case of almost all of us, is immediately to feel and to try to do something. There is this fact of limited sympathy, a part of our human nature. David Hume of the eighteenth century, best of British philosophers, possibly of philosophers, made it a foundation of his account of morality.

Out of these three facts of desire, consistency and sympathy, morality arises, or so it can seem. It has seemed so, in different ways, to various philosophers. To a few philosophers it has seemed to arise out of just one of the three facts, at any rate with a little help. It was Hume's predecessor Thomas Hobbes who said that our selfish natures, if we did not restrain them by entering into self-denying agreements with others, would result in our lives being 'solitary, poor, nasty, brutish, and short'. In effect, this explains morality as being the result of just the first fact about us, self-interest, along with the rationality distinguished from the simple consistency talked about above – the rationality of choosing means to ends properly and wisely.

But surely what would issue from only a calculation of self-interest, without any influence of sympathy with others generally, would not be a full or standard morality. A standard morality is more than collaborative self-interest. An agreed system of laws, conventions, rules, rights and so on, whether or not they were also given legal expression, if it was all collaborative self-interest and contained nothing about the Korean child, no general sympathy, would only uncertainly be a morality.

Do you wish to rewrite this point in a certain low or very realistic way? Do you insist that morality is no more than a mutually satisfactory agreement, and point out that the mentioned wider sympathy or benevolence is exactly something that a shrewd party to such an agreement will put into it? Do you note that if a question arises of my trying to satisfy my selfish desires by abandoning our rules and attacking you, I am less likely to do so if the morality we share is not only an entirely self-serving agreement – if I know you have some sympathy with me? I have no great objection to this lowness. What is essential, and not in dispute between us, is that a morality has in it something more than self-interest plainly or narrowly conceived. It has in it some degree of what it remains natural to call sympathy.

This stands in some connection with what was said of reasons above. It has a source in and can be expected to exist because of the fact that when I claim something for myself, I have a reason. In almost all cases, whether or not I actually give my reason, it is discernible by others. Suppose it is that I am hungry. It is then open to anyone else to put in for food on the same basis, and claim my support. My reason also justifies him in his hunger. So he says. Maybe he adds that the reason in fact is a *principle* to the effect that the hungry are to get food.

Of course, if the situation is one of some scarcity, and we are not saints, each of us is likely to advance further reasons. I may say he may be hungry but the food is my private property. He may say he has to be able to work to keep his family together, which I do not. But our greater and common reason, hunger, will still exist. It may seem stronger than any other reason. This is another part of the explanation of the fact that morality arguably goes beyond or is led beyond being a self-interested arrangement. People we don't know can try to make use of our strongest reasons, and we know this. In particular they can also try to make use of those large reasons applicable to many cases – principles.

None of this needs to deny that morality does also have feelings in it that are different from humanity or compassion. Some of us feel very strongly, as we say, that people *deserve* penalties for what they have done. To say the least, this is not a case of a feeling *for* others, not sympathy or the like. The feeling expressed in the retribution theory of the justification of punishment is not a matter of fellow-feeling. Nor is the feeling of resolution in the deterrence theory of punishment a matter of sympathy with the person being punished. But these feelings mainly have to do in different ways with the self-interest. They also have to do, of course, with sympathy for people generally – the victims of offenders.

More to natural morality, and its inescapability

The story up to here is that the natural fact and practice of morality is collaborative self-interest, taking in the interest of one's own family and the like, along with some sympathy for everyone else, and that it is a matter of having reasons for things and therefore of consistency. More particularly, the natural fact and practice of morality consists in attitudes describable in terms of the cooperative self-interest, and the sympathy and the reasons, which attitudes have as their content or are expressed in judgements on actions and persons, in claims of moral rights, and in rules, principles and the like.

The judgements, claims of moral rights and obligations and so on do not form a systematic whole. They are different from something else to which we shall be attending, workings-out of what ordinary morality does come to or ought to come to, the labours of philosophers and moralists, in the past with the aid of religion. These are usually recommended selections or enlargements of particular principles or other elements of natural morality.

The attitudes, judgements and the like, and also the worked-out moralities by philosophers and others, have to do with right actions, with moral approval or disapproval for them, maybe issuing in praise or blame, and with moral standing over a lifetime or part of one. The attitudes, judgements and the like, and the systematized or anyway reflective moralities, give rise to the law of the land, what is legal, and subsequently judge it and in due course alter and transform it.

In fact, the attitudes issue in judgement on everything. That is not to say they are as clear and determinate as a clear-headed fellow would like. Furthermore they are not themselves in perfect consistency. They can pull in different directions. The self-interest may not always sit well with the rationality. Neither of these may always sit well with the sympathy. Nor is that the only complication.

It would be agreeable to think that these attitudes were entirely a natural growth, hardy perennials, developing on their own by themselves, owed only to what is in common between us. That is a comforting idea to some of us, but it cannot be the case. Karl Marx was only one student of our societies who saw, to put the point traditionally, that our morality is to some extent shaped by a ruling class, if not very conspiratorially, in order to keep the lower orders more in order. Friedrich Engels learned from him his saying that all morality is class morality. The more clubbable John Stuart Mill, also of the nineteenth century, said something along the same lines in *On Liberty*. The emphasis on the right of private property is a large part of this management of our morality.

If that grubbiness needs to be fitted in, there is also another thing to the fact and practice of morality. If this does not make it simpler either, it is something unembarrassing, and a long way from Marx and Engels.

Morality, as just remarked, has strong feelings in it, including feelings about others than oneself and close persons. Some more of these feelings are about children and sex offenders, torture, starvation, the Holocaust, and the refugee camps at Sabra, Shatilla and Jenin. These feelings are so strong as to seem to be facts. Or, to speak more carefully, they seem to be of facts, reports on facts. Not just to someone who passionately believes something in particular, but at least to very many of us. There seem to be *general* facts, perhaps of still greater importance. To see this you need an unrealistically uncomplicated example.

Imagine a man in a strange situation. He knows only one thing, as we do, about pressing the button that is in front of him – that it would cause suffering but would be safe for him. He does not believe anything else at all about pressing the button. He does not know or think anything about who or what will suffer if he presses it, or about their past, or about any further effect of their suffering. Nothing about good results of any kind, such as the prevention of greater suffering. Nor does he believe anything about satisfactions or other feelings he himself will have if he presses the button.

Imagine he *does* press it, with understanding, and not as any kind of unbelieving performance. Are you reluctant to say it is *true* in the plainest sense that he did something wrong? Do you say that while you of course agree that what he did was wrong, this is not *as true* as the statement that you are reading this sentence? That it does not literally correspond to a fact? Your reluctance may be owed to a common idea about moral utterances just expressing the way someone feels about something. It may be owed to what you may hear, whatever it can mean, from someone of advanced or alternative views, that your particular moral beliefs are *true for you*. Your reluctance can also have a source in philosophical views that take moral utterances as not being true or false but merely urgings, exhortations or attempts to command.

That is all very well. But you will still agree, I trust, about the man who presses the button, that his doing so establishes *some* pretty plain truth along certain lines: that his action is that of someone mad, less than human, deranged at the moment, or something of that sort. It is not just that we don't *like* it and him. This isn't just subjectivity or attitudes.

There are other such examples. What of the woman who knows *only* that pressing the button in front of her will end a situation in which two people have just barely enough to eat, and in future will give more of that total amount to one of them? Remember she knows only that. This reflection, like the previous one, can persuade you that even if morality has more than one element or side, and is complicated and disputed, there are facts in it or at the bottom of it.

We can but note this large matter that has been at the heart of much moral philosophy. It seems to have not only attitudes but some real facts in it. We must look at something else quickly. Given what has been said, is morality optional? The question has got attention from philosophers, starting with Plato. Some have certainly seemed to suppose it *is* optional, since that is implied by another question that is asked and does seem to make sense – 'Why be moral?'

In fact morality is inescapable. What this means, of course, is that it is owed to and called up by our common desires. It is in our interest, required by our instrumental rationality, more in the interest of some of us. It is also in accord with our natures as sympathetic. It is as it is, further, because of our rationality in the sense having to do with reasons and consistency. Plainly there are those among us who depart from our self-interested agreement as far as possible. In terms of the costs and benefits of the system, they do not pay the first and do take the second. We cannot all join them, or we lose the benefits. We need the system and so we do what we can to stop their number from getting too large.

Worked-out moralities

So much for the nature of the fact and practice of morality, a sprawling and somewhat uncertain fact, and too little for those truths that seem to be in it. Do you have the idea that we have not taken the shortest distance between two points? That we should have gone straight to the matter of the principles that come out of the fact and practice, worked-out principles by philosophers and the like that claim to clarify it, define it rightly, advance or reform it, and may also be attempts to advance particular causes or interests?

I doubt it. Our thinking about terrorism and its sources, say in good articles on comment pages in good newspapers, sometimes has and certainly should have a particular uncertainty about it – as to morality in general, the sort of thing it is. Our thinking runs into the question of what sort of thing we have been offending against in helping to give rise to, if we have, circumstances of deprivation that have to do with the subsequent terrorism. It is necessary neither to overstate nor to understate the nature of morality in this connection. Its nature is as relevant to our condemnation of terrorism and to our judgements on responses of our governments to it.

Let us now come closer to the question of what worked-out moral principles to bring to bear on ourselves, on September 11 and other possible and conceivable terrorism, and on what we are to do. These will be principles of wider relevance, and what strength they have will be owed partly to that fact. They will indeed be general answers to the question of what is right – what actions, practices and institutions are right. They will be general answers to the question of moral rights and obligations in any particular society or nation – how things are to be in it. They will also be very relevant to the question of relations between societies, but we will leave explicit consideration of that until the following stages of our inquiry.

As already noted, these moral principles about right actions, practices and institutions seem to give rise to or anyway stand in connection with other judgements (p. 7, p. 9). Certainly there are implications in both directions, if not so simple as might be expected. We take people to be responsible for things, the human causes of them, and we go beyond that to hold them responsible or credit them with responsibility. That is, we disapprove or approve of them morally with respect to particular actions and their intentions in them, and of course effects of the actions. To do this is, among other things, to take the action as against or in accord with a principle or principles of right action.

Natural and other morality

We also make more general judgements on persons and their standings or characters. As used to be asked, what is it to be a good man, a virtuous man? Better, who is human or decent? Who is not to be shaken hands with? And, to remember that morality and even worked-out morality is part of all life, as much now as in the past, who has shown himself to be a shit in how he has lived?

Some moral philosophers have started with the third subject, asking what characters we should or should not have, what virtues or good personal dispositions as against vices we should have, rather than what actions are right. They *do* allow that morality is fundamentally about what to do, not about what sort of character to be or credit or blame, but they have assumed that you get to right principles of action by thinking about the virtues that express them – say a man's disposition to justice.

It is, to say the least, hard to discern the advantage of this roundabout procedure. Certainly we commonly condemn an action as wrong by saying it was the action of a man of no decency or honour, or by holding him morally responsible for it, disapproving of him for it. But we commonly do so because of the action, surely. In that case, why start elsewhere?

Other philosophers, more challenging, have gone against assumptions made so far. They have said that there can be no valid moral principles as to what actions are right and wrong – nothing really general and useful – and so what we need to think about is the temperate man or the just man or whatever, maybe he who *sees* what is right in a particular situation. That is not my inclination, and it is not widely shared.

What sufficient reason is there for thinking that there are no general and useful answers to the question of what is right or just or fair? They need not be eternal truths, of course, or such as to procure universal agreement. They need to be clear, to recommend themselves, and to be arguable and reasonably defensible among parties to a discussion. Their definiteness, against the indefiniteness of moralities having to do with such virtues or character-dispositions as justice and love, enables us to see what we do think and feel.

Thus a principle, even if not an indubitable principle, is a better means of arriving at a judgement about the right action than, say, stuff from the ancient philosopher Aristotle about the Golden Mean – about how the man of good character is not intemperate in any direction and is moved to act to the right degree on the right occasion for the right reason with respect to the right people. Didn't we know that already, by the way?

If there were no general principles of what is right and wrong, then we would need to try to give up the endeavour of consistency. If there were no general principles to bring to bear on different cases, then there would be no common standard for judging them. It would be like trying to compare sizes of shoes without having common units of measurement. There would be no way of seeing if we were being in the most fundamental sense reasonable. If there were no general principles we would need to try to give up a lot. We would need to try to give up part of our nature, our rationality of consistency or much of it.

So let us look quickly at three sets of such principles, three answers to the question of how we should further define and shape the natural fact and practice of morality – shape the attitudes that are in our general interest, more in the interest of some of us, and are in a way rational, and have some sympathy for strangers in them, and some sort of plain truth.

Libertarianism

The first set of principles has contributed as much as any other in the past quarter-century to the ongoing process of defining and shaping. It has passed a test of time. It has contributed to the articulated outlooks preferred by several governments and administrations, not to mention a lot of their associated businessmen, notably those who are happy to speak of their capitalism – to which thing we will have to pay some attention sooner or later.

Like the other two sets of principles, as already anticipated, it is primarily a worked-out social morality – a prescription for a society, an account of the good or the just society. It also has implications for relations between societies, about which we have a lot less moral theory. Insofar as it can be distinct, it is not primarily a worked-out morality for private life. It is the work of Robert Nozick, laid out in his book *Anarchy, State and Utopia*, not enlighteningly titled. The anarchy from Harvard is not what some progressive students in Wisconsin may have expected.

The book was taken as raising political philosophers from dogmatic slumbers. Part of the slumbering, if such it was, was the habit of taking individuals in a society to be no more than possible receivers of satisfactions, possible possessors of the great goods. In short, desirers. The moral philosophy of Utilitarianism, in the nineteenth century the work of Jeremy Bentham and John Stuart Mill, comes to mind first. No doubt it seemed to them exactly the doctrine or principle suggested by the nature of morality, but there is room for doubt.

Their Principle of Utility is to the effect that the right action is the one that is likely, on the best available information and judgement, to produce the greatest total of satisfaction, misleadingly called the greatest happiness of the greatest number. The best society is the one that acts to do this. Unfortunately, as many have said, it seems this could be a society with some slaves in it, or some victims of other kinds, since it is conceivable that such a society would be happier in total than the alternatives. But I stray – that is not the present point. It is that Utilitarianism does indeed look at individuals only in terms of certain of their qualities, their being satisfiable creatures.

Something of the same sort is the case with a morality summed up by the maxim 'To each according to their needs', say for food. Other very different social moralities, including elitist ones, have also been in favour of distributing things according to qualities possessed by individuals. Things are to go to individuals according to their moral desert, whatever that means, or some kind of cultural or intellectual excellence, or their productivity, or their efforts. Like Utilitarianism, these moralities see a certain pattern of qualities in persons as they now are, or as they recently have been, and propose to follow the pattern in giving things out to the persons.

All of these moralities may seem oblivious to something else. These are not actual qualities of individuals or the like, but *entitlements*.

The facts of entitlements do not have to do with the pattern of qualities now, but are about something else in a lot more of the past. Things have a history. The things that are our means to the great goods have a history. The history of these means is fundamental to the issue of who ought and who ought not to possess them now. Things are in the right places, possessed by the right people, if they have come to them out of a certain past. They must have a history in accord with certain conditions, in fact two or three principles.

Think of some land, conceivably yours around your summer cottage. At some past time, it first came into ownership, became a piece of private property. Whoever came to own it, he was in fact entitled to it if he mixed his labour with the land, and if it was also true that by coming to own it, he did not worsen the situation of others around him. Here was an instance of *justice in first acquisition*. Talk of mixing labour with something, not only land, comes from John Locke in the seventeenth century, and remains tempting. Suppose now that the property changed hands in a proper way. It was sold, inherited, maybe given away. What is important is that the change in ownership was *voluntary* – it was chosen or agreed to by both parties. It was thus an instance of *justice in transfer*. Suppose too that it went on being justly transferred right up to your acquiring it.

Let us now think a lot more generally, about a society where *every* thing in it that is owned has a history like that of your piece of land. It started out in the right way, and at no point was an owner forced to give it up, or cheated out of it, or deprived of it by having it stolen from him. Nor was it or any part of it appropriated in any other way without his agreement, say by the state or government imposing an inheritance tax. Every transfer of every item had the indubitable recommendation of being a matter of full voluntariness. It follows that the society is perfectly just, that it is right and proper, that everyone has what he or she has a right to.

This is not at all a proposition about legality and legal rights. The question we are contemplating, and Professor Nozick's question, is not about a society's legal correctness, whatever that would be. It is about moral rights, of what legal rights there *ought* to be in any society, of what ought to be done or ought not to be done, what is morally obligatory and what isn't. The answer we have is to the effect that a morally just society, which of course will have to have certain laws, is one in accord with the two principles. Alternatively, to add a third point, it can be a just society even if something *was* transferred without agreement at some point in history, but the situation was then rectified – somehow put back to what it would have been if the involuntary transfer had not happened.

The recommendation of this society is in what is called the evident liberty of it, including liberty from what may be called government interference. This society will only involve a minimal state. The recommendation of it can be shown explicitly by a comparison with your own different conception of the just society, perhaps one that is more equal in income and wealth, perhaps a more utopian one.

Imagine that your own just society comes about, and that it has Wilt Chamberlain in it, a wonderful basketball player. He is willing to go on playing, but only for some extra money, and the fans are willing to pay it. They are willing to make him rich. The only way that your egalitarian society can be kept going is by getting in the way of this transaction – by denying liberty. Only Professor Nozick's ideal society does not rest on infringing our liberty.

This libertarianism has reflected something in our societies and been part of a good deal of similar thinking that has influenced them. Thus it is of some relevance to the question of our contribution to the state of things in other societies, and to hostility in them towards us, and to our thinking about that hostility. What is to be said about this libertarianism? What is to be said about its perfectly just society? Certainly the doctrine is a reminder that a just society will pay attention to claims arising out of the recent and maybe the less recent past. But does Utilitarianism, for example, really not do that? Does it not count in the satisfaction of your keeping what you have a legal right to? Bentham and Mill would be very surprised by the idea, but forget about all that.

The main answer to the question of what is to be said about this libertarianism can be seen by thinking about some persons starving to death in its perfectly just society. Certainly there can be such persons even though everything is exactly where it ought to be in terms of the history. Each thing, every means to well-being, is owned by exactly the right person or family or corporation. Nothing has gone wrong with all that – it's just that the starving persons or their parents have been feckless, unintelligent, on drugs, in bad health, had crippling accidents, or something of the sort.

The simple fact to think about is that in this perfectly just society they have no claim to food, no moral right to it. No one and nothing does wrong in letting them starve to death. There is no obligation in this society, on the state or anything or anyone else, to save them from starving to death. It is not true of anyone that he or she ought to have helped them.

This is vicious. Nothing, certainly not a philosopher's playful speculativeness in laying it out, will make this conception of the just society less than that. Nor, remembering that there seems to be some plain truth in morality, am I inclined merely to say that it is vicious *to me*. Those words were written before Professor Nozick died, in January 2002, leaving behind him grateful students and many philosophical admirers, not all of them supporters of his politics. He was a clever man. But my words had better stand. There are things that are more important than not speaking ill of the dead.

In order to pretend that libertarianism is in fact a possible reshaping of our natural morality, it may have added to it that there is room in the just society as conceived for charity. This charity, it can be said, recognizes and is the manifestation of the generalized sympathy for others that is part of the fact of natural morality. There are answers to this. That generalized concern in natural morality is not merely the attitude that one *might* intervene, out of a good heart, but one does no wrong at all in letting others die of starvation right there when this could easily have been prevented. And the contemplated charity in libertarianism is no significant recommendation, being cheap and optional, these being its real recommendations.

This libertarianism, then, lets people starve to death and supposes we have no obligation at all to help them go on living. There are related objections having to do with people being denied any of the other great goods and the items within them. Being taught to read comes to mind.

It can come as no surprise that the pieces of thinking that result in the right and proper libertarian society appear to be open to objection.

We do not hear *why* it is that my mixing my labour with something hitherto unowned, which is to say working on it, gives me a right to it. Certainly it's a question. There *is* the playful joke made that maybe pouring a can of tomato juice into the ocean gives you ownership of the ocean. That leaves the question untouched. It needs to be touched. Working on something may indeed give you a right to it, but doesn't the reason for this actually have to do with *fairness* or something of the sort, maybe fair compensation for your labour? John Locke had this kind of thing in mind. But then, later on, can unlucky children not put in for property on the same basis? If there's nothing available for them to mix their labour with, doesn't something have to be done by the society?

Is there a recommendation for *any* voluntary exchange between persons? Plainly not. No recommendation at all attaches to your voluntarily giving me the gun you know will be used by me to shoot my wife. What recommendation attaches to a voluntary sale that will deprive a peasant village of the jobs that were its only means of support up until now? Clearly, it is only *some* exchanges that are recommended by their voluntariness. In which case, the history of the just society has been left entirely incomplete. There is the probability, indeed the certainty, that whatever could be added in to legitimize or give a recommendation to transfers, whatever moral reason, could also be used in favour of some redistribution of goods later on.

Wilt Chamberlain. We have it that to prevent him from disturbing, say, the equality of a society, would infringe the liberty of himself and the fans. What is a liberty? Is there a liberty to murder or rape? Rob banks? There is not. To have a liberty in the relevant sense, whatever else it comes to, is to be able to act in a way that has a recommendation or justification. You have to have a right. Suppose for a moment that the good public health system in the equal society may in the end be endangered by the precedent of the transaction between Wilt and the fans. A question must arise about

45

the recommendation of the transaction, which is to say a question must arise about their having a liberty to do the thing. All the necessary argument for the supposed liberty is missing.

This libertarianism is barely what we have so far allowed it to be, a working-out or the like of our natural morality. Despite any thoughts about charity, it is nearly a defeat of natural morality, a replacement of it by something else. This is not only a matter having to do with our sympathy for people not connected to us. This libertarianism cannot be counted on to serve our interests, even the interests of a majority. It gives too much to too few, too little to too many, and so endangers the agreement that is at the bottom of natural morality. It is sad that it has had some indirect effect on impressionable politicians whose official political traditions should have preserved them from it.

It is, by the way, not so new a doctrine as often supposed. It is in fact an expression of a long tradition, a kind of conservatism. Edmund Burke, he of the eighteenth century who damned the French Revolution and discoursed on the sublime and the beautiful, is sometimes taken as the father of conservatism in general, or conservatism in English-speaking places. He had an opinion about the obligation of the British government with respect to the impoverished Irish under them who were starving. The obligation of the British government, he said, went no further than offering to sell them food.

You need not agree with me about him or about libertarianism – we can go forward together in this inquiry anyway. In the end your conclusions or doubts can rest on exactly a denial of what your guide takes to be obvious. You can learn from what seem to you to be my mistakes, maybe my want of realism. Still, I have confidence that not many of us will side with libertarianism. Will more be in favour of something else?

Liberalism

What we can call liberalism is expressed in *A Theory of Justice*, by John Rawls. It too comes from Harvard, and it too has lasted. Nothing as large has succeeded it. In the last twenty-five years it has had more attention from political philosophers than any other answer to the question of how our societies ought to be, partly because of the argument advanced for it.

The root idea in the argument is that what is right is what people would agree to in a fair situation. Think about some people making a contract between themselves for the society they are setting up, settling the principles that will govern it. The people have five characteristics, the last of them exceptional.

1. Each of them is self-interested.
2. They are also equal in putting up proposals as to the right principles.
3. Each is rational in the sense of choosing effective and economical means to the possession of what are called primary goods, and is not envious.
4. They are said to have a lot of *general* knowledge – would it be better to say general beliefs? – about human psychology, society, politics and economics.
5. Most importantly, each is absolutely ignorant of his or her *individual* future in the society to come. None knows if he or she will be long-lived or not, rich or poor, shrewd or otherwise, of this race or that, of a particular social or economic class, male or female, of this or that moral outlook or religion, and so on.

The idea in the contract argument, more particularly, is that the social principles that would be agreed on by these imagined people are the right ones for *our* actual societies today – the United States, Germany and so on. If you think this odd, you might contemplate that an absolutely fair agreement-making situation *has* to be an imaginary one. In life as it is, you don't get the right conditions. Thus that the situation is imaginary in no way reduces the real recommendation for us of what is chosen.

What would the people in question agree on? Not any racist principle, clearly, since each of them faces the possibility of being black or brown. As clearly, they would not choose the libertarian principles just noticed. Or Utilitarianism. What they would choose,

47

in effect, or so it is argued, are three principles of justice. They are ranked or ordered principles, the first has priority if there is conflict with the other two, the second to have priority if there is conflict with the third.

The first principle is about certain liberties, and is that each person in the society is to have the greatest amount of these rights that is consistent with everybody else having the same. These liberties include political rights, freedom of the person, freedom of thought and expression, and the right to hold private property.

The second principle, like the third principle, is about socio-economic inequalities or differences. The second principle is that if there are any such inequalities, there is to be a considerable equality of opportunity to get into the upper or better positions. If the society has millionaires and billionaires in it, everybody will have a kind of chance of becoming one.

The third principle is that there are only to be, but there are to be, any inequalities that make the worst-off class better-off than they would be in the absence of those inequalities. What this comes to, more or less, is that some people are to be rich if that makes the poor less poor – if there is that effect, as some say, because goods trickle down to the poor.

It's a decent outlook, isn't it? Reassures you about Harvard? Makes you happier, if you're English, that America is now Rome to England's Greece? Reconciles you to the imperial ascendancy of American philosophers? Maybe it does so even though questions come up, the first of them about the argument for it, the contract argument.

The contractors agree on principles that have to do with a certain amount or degree of equality, in both opportunity and socio-economic goods. Pass by the question of how much equality for a minute. They also agree on some amount or institution of private property for their society to come. If you think about it, these agreements must be owed to the fact that the contractors have certain beliefs. Their mentioned general beliefs must contain certain beliefs in particular. They must have beliefs that boil down to this: the given amount of equality and private property have good effects in a society.

They could be right about this, but they could be wrong. A libertarian in favour of very extensive and strong private property rights will probably disagree with the contractors. But the point is not that the libertarian is right – or that average voters, social democrats, socialists or remaining communists would be right in disagreeing with the contractors. The point, which has been made elsewhere before now, is that our going along with the contract argument, in effect taking the original contractors as good guides for our societies, presupposes that *they* are right about the extent of equality in a society and the private-property rights. So the contract argument seems to begin with or assume what it is supposed to prove. It gets out at the end what it quietly put in without reason at the beginning.

It's a circular argument, then, and it brings to mind that you could devise other contract arguments. Fidel Castro could have worked one out for Cuba, couldn't he? Maybe he did. There is another point, smaller but piquant.

You may have been thinking, naturally enough, that the contractors are different from one another, that they bring different judgements and outlooks to the business. In fact they don't – they have to be thought of as having the very same properties, just the properties one to five. They have to be thought of that way if there is to be a chance of really arguing that they will agree on the given principles of liberalism rather than anything else. Who knows what a motley collection of characters would agree on? Professor Rawls to his credit accepts this. So is there exactly as much recommendation in this agreement or contract coming about as there is in something else: my agreeing or contracting with myself?

Of course the three principles could be perfectly OK, even if the given argument for them is hopeless. That can happen. There are bad arguments for the world's being round. Are the principles OK?

It is a little hard to see what they come to. According to the liberty principle, what is to be shared out equally at the highest possible level is not political power, or actually getting a hearing for opinions, or actual private property or whatever. It is not such powers or possessions that are to be equal, as is made clear, but *rights* to them.

It is best to think of legal rights. So what the principle says at bottom is that the law will not obstruct any particular individuals or classes in the given respects. There will be no law against any class of people getting elected or on television or rich.

What will the result of this be? We know about the rights, but what actual powers and possessions and so on are we talking about in this connection? What actual distribution of these things is to have priority over any redistribution of goods that might happen under the third principle, about socio-economic inequalities? Could the actual powers and possessions be those that go with the top tenth of the population having 30.5 per cent of the total income or consumption and the bottom tenth 1.8 per cent? Those were the American figures in that table (p. 8).

This uncertainty has another side to it. We can divide all the resources in liberalism's just society into two parts. The first part falls under the control or operation of the liberties principle. The second part falls under the principles about equal opportunity and socio-economic differences. The resources in the latter part will provide opportunities, possibly special schools. Maybe even more important, these will be resources that can be redistributed if it turns out that less inquality will make a worst-off class better-off. But how much is there in this part of the pie? Does most of the pie in fact turn out to be private property defended and made sacrosanct by the liberty principle? Is there much left for the egalitarian good work? Who knows? Not me.

There is another problem, one that bothers me still more. It has to do with the egalitarian good work, the third principle. You may have been counting on that. A good society is to have *as much* inequality or incentive as actually benefits a worst-off class. It is easy to think that that is pretty definite, but is it? *As much* inequality as benefits a worst-off class. Until we are told more, that could be no inequality at all, or as much as anybody can think of. It could be the top tenth of population having 30.5 per cent and the bottom tenth 1.8 per cent, or just about any other shares you can think of.

Pretty clearly, something is missing at this point. It is an answer to the question of how much inequality we actually need or are to be taken to need, in order to do the job. Is it as much as the better-off have now? Something like this seems to be assumed. But it is odd, to say the least, anyway in a political philosophy, just to take the demands of the better-off as they are. As *givens*, not to be looked at. After all, they are as self-interested as the rest of us, and pretty good at looking after themselves.

Is there an answer in economics to this question? There sure isn't. The whole subject in its relevant part is an ongoing dispute about such a question. This is a dispute caught up in the larger issue we are considering – how a society ought to be, what principles ought to govern it, what the just society is. Economics in this part, whatever else it is, is disguised politics. Adam Smith, friend of Hume, started it when he said that if everyone in a society pursues their own profit and nothing else, it is as if a hidden hand makes things work out for the best. Is it that way? You wouldn't guess it from the state of the British railways in 2001 after they were privatized.

The short story about this liberalism, to my mind, is mainly that it is a matter of good intentions not carried into clear definitions. To my mind it shares the besetting sin of all liberalisms and something called pluralism. Also the English stuff with the name of *The Third Way*. That has been the philosophy of my own party, New Labour. Mr Blair's philosophy, but still a kind of bumble that gives sociology a bad name. It is not clear politics.

After hearing a lot, and thinking about the contract argument, you're left in the dark as to what this liberalism really comes to, the bottom lines. To go back to the 30.5 per cent and the 1.8 per cent in the table, could it be that the whole thing is an announcement that America is OK? The right sort of society? Could we have saved some time in getting to that conclusion? Was there a shorter distance between two points? Hard to say.

The principle of humanity

That may be one reason for looking at something different, a third social morality, something worked out by me before now, and in different ways by a lot of predecessors. An early one of those was

Colonel Rainborough, who said something true in the Putney Debates at the time of the English Civil War in the seventeenth century. 'Really I think that the poorest he that is in England hath a life to live as the greatest he ...' Something like the same note was sounded in the recollection fourscore and seven years later of 'a new nation, conceived in liberty, and dedicated to the proposition that all men are created equal'. Abraham Lincoln, he who freed slaves, 1863.

Another reason for looking at this different social morality is that you may take it to be not only better than liberalism, but right. It may be most in line with natural morality too, which is not to say perfectly in line. Also, it may be the social morality most relevant to the subject of terrorism. It may provide the best basis for judging it, perhaps for condemning it. It may also, whether or not paradoxically, be closest to the outlook of actual and possible terrorists and those who sympathize with them, or as they say, *understand* them.

At bottom it is simple. Its subject-matter, so to speak, has already had your attention – great goods and bad lives. We can move quickly.

To enumerate the goods again, they were:

1. a decent length of life,
2. a quality of life owed to such material means as fillings for teeth,
3. freedom and power, certainly including what the Palestinians lack,
4. respect and self-respect, including what is lacked by workers paid hardly anything for the profitable stuff they produce but afraid to form a union,
5. relationships both personal and as members of smaller and larger groups,
6. a culture or way of living, including the tradition of a people and a language, and knowledge in place of ignorance.

As for bad lives, you may remember that the question of an exact definition of a bad life was passed by when we were looking at facts of short lives (p. 20). It was then clear enough for our purposes to say that a life can be bad because it is a half-life or a quarter-life, or because of lacking other things.

Natural and other morality

Is there a question of fact, of plain truth and falsehood, as to exactly what lives are bad? Many or most of us are inclined to say no – it's a matter of opinion or feeling. Some of us take this thought as reason for a kind of complacency. Whether or not we should be complacent, there certainly is a question here. It is an instance of the uncertainty there is about the nature of morality – the extent to which it has real truth in it. It does seem clear enough that the general definition of bad lives is *more* a matter of decision than discovery, more a matter of personal judgement than of plain truth. My judgement is as follows.

Lives are bad if they are cut short – half-lives, quarter-lives and still shorter lives. So are lives bad, not that there can be many of them, that are long enough but have in them no significant amount of the material goods that make for physical well-being. Lives are bad, thirdly, if they lack the great satisfaction of freedom, power and safety. Denials of political and other rights to a people in a home-land, as in Palestine and to a lesser extent in Ireland, come here, and also wars, attacks, and severely damaging economic domination.

A life is bad, fourthly, if it is deprived of what we all want, a human standing. If it were possible to have a life not bad in any of the mentioned ways, but devoid of respect and self-respect, it would still be a bad life. It was no good being a nigger. It still isn't. So too, fifthly and finally, is a life bad if it is long enough but has in it but little of all the other great goods.

Let me here pass by your reaction, if you have it, that this general definition in its five parts is arbitrary. Let us also pass by my response that any arbitrariness will be a general fact of our moral thinking, and of your thinking about mine in particular.

Instead, let me go on to state the third social morality, a morality of humanity, fellow-feeling, or generosity. This has in it one fundamental principle. This principle of humanity is that what we need to do morally is to try to save people from bad lives – this is the stuff of our moral obligations and rights. You will want some details. OK, the principle is that the right thing to do is the one that according to the best judgement and information is the rational thing with respect to the end or goal of saving people from bad lives. The rational thing, in this sense, is of course the one that probably will be effective with respect to the goal and also economical as against self-defeating – it will not give rise to more bad lives than it ends or prevents.

What we need to try to do, more specifically, is to reduce the number of bad lives by certain policies. These have to do not only with those who have or will have bad lives, *the badly-off*, as we can call them, but also the remainder who have good lives, *the better-off*.

The first policy is to rescue the badly-off by means that do not significantly affect the well-being of the better-off. Indubitably such means exist, and more will or can come into existence. If this policy by itself would do the trick, that would be the end of the matter. The aim of this social morality is not to drag people down.

That remains true despite the second policy, which in fact is needed. This second policy is transferring means from the better-off that *do* significantly affect their well-being – without making them badly-off. Real redistribution. In the world as we have it, this is fundamental.

A third policy of this resolute humanity has to do with something that will come to mind in connection with the second, and came up with liberalism. It is the proposition that taking something away from the lives of the better-off, maybe a lot, will reduce their incentives to contribute to the whole social pie of means to well-being, and thereby have exactly the wrong effect – make people badly-off. On no subject in the world, you can sometimes feel, is more nonsense and cant to be heard.

The third policy, unlike anything noticeable in liberalism, takes into account that to require or demand rewards of certain kinds is a matter of the attitude of the person in question. The policy, to state it, is to reduce incentive-inequalities to really necessary ones – ones of which it is really true, and not just a convenient assumption, that to get rid of them would actually reduce the total means to well-being.

The fourth policy is implicit in the three we have but needs to be made explicit. It has most to do with the great goods of freedom, power and safety, and is a prohibition on wounding, attack, killing, torture, sexual attack and violation, threat, intimidation, and other violence and near-violence. Since this policy cannot rule out the use of force by all societies against individuals, and also an individual's right of self-defence, and action in extremity, the definition of the policy is not easy. We will in a way return to the matter (p. 118).

It needs adding that the principle of humanity in its fullness is not only to the effect that actually effective policies are to be embraced to change and prevent bad lives, but also that we have certain practices of *equality* that will help. One is the democratic practice, widely realized, of one person, one vote. Another is the practice, far from realized and certainly as important, of an equality among all political parties and candidates with respect to their finances. We will come back to this, but you will anticipate that the principle is not actually in favour of your being able to *buy* the office of mayor of New York. Other practices of equality do not have to do with politics but with common situations of equal need, such as hunger.

More could be said to fill out the principle, and to try to answer questions that arise, as in the case of the libertarian and liberal principles. It will not need saying, in connection with the second and third policies, that this humanitarianism is not so speculative as to speculate, with Professor Nozick, that paying taxes on what you earn from your work is on a par with forced labour. But a little essay could be written on the extent to which the principle respects expectations on the part of owners of private property, and also on the part of those who benefit from established rights in our existing moralities and our panoply of beliefs about human nature and societies.

As you may gather, the idea is neither to disdain these legal entitlements and benefits nor to take them as sacrosanct. We will get around to the subject of capitalism and all that, but to put a bit more definition on the principle of humanity now, let me remark that a supporter of it could go wrong in taking resources from the better-off. A property-owner could wrongly be made badly-off precisely by the distress of having expectations deriving from legal rights frustrated.

That may not reassure you enough. Do you have in mind that familiar accusation or reprimand both to certain moralities and kinds of political action – that they take the end to justify the means? Do you say that the second and third policies in overriding rights and expectations take the end to justify the means? It is not clear what the accusation ever comes to. Bertrand Russell, a better philosopher than some others in Cambridge in the early part of the last century, on hearing that someone or something took the end to justify the means, asked what else could. There is sense in that reply, but it is not what needs to be said.

Someone is accused of the offence when he is willing to go against the rights of some individuals, or to make things less good for them, in order to achieve the end, as he says, of very many individuals having *their* moral rights, maybe longer lives. In what way, exactly, is he supposed to go wrong? If he is a supporter of the principle of humanity, certainly it cannot be by his allowing that *any* means is justified in order to secure the end. As you will remember about this humanity as defined, its second policy limits what is to be transferred from the better-off to the badly-off. The better-off are not to be made badly-off themselves. This humanitarianism does not come near to tolerating *any* means. It does not justify anything like the victimization that wrecks Utilitarianism (p. 41).

The accusation raises other questions, it seems to me, but all that it can come to is the proposition that we would be wrong to reduce what can properly be called the excess well-being of some or a few in order to have very many more come up to a minimum level of well-being. *Why* would that be wrong? That it would be wrong is the *conclusion* of the objector, not a reason for the conclusion. We were to be getting a reason, weren't we?

The principle of humanity, as it also seems to me, has been at the bottom of the English tradition of egalitarianism, an American counterpart, and broader currents of fellow-feeling and generosity. It has been at the bottom of the egalitarianisms, and partly for that reason called the principle of equality in the past, despite the fact that it is a principle about people having bad lives, as distinct from lives unequal to other lives. Bad lives were the real concern, very arguably, of the traditions of egalitarianism. But in any case the principle of humanity is about distress and suffering, not a relation between people – which fact is consistent with the truth that to succeed in implementing it would be to make people more equal.

Do you ask for a formal argument for the principle? Haven't you had enough of those in connection with social moralities? Think back. Maybe you should suppose instead that at bottom a moral principle recommends itself. As previous pages have indicated, along with the whole history of moral reflection and moral philosophy, proofs in morality have not been attained. It is possible to wonder whether they really have some other use – reassuring those who are believers already. That is not to say that nothing can be said for the principle of humanity.

The main thing is that each of us wants things, and has reasons for having them. This is fundamental to the fact and practice of our natural morality. Other people can take over our reason for their own use. We can resist them by offering further reasons, making distinctions. My prospect of hunger, I say, is in this or that way to be accorded a standing or importance larger than yours. I am different in this special way – on account of my entitlements or whatever. These new reasons, if they do remain within morality, have the ring of selfishness about them. The principle of humanity or fellow-feeling does not. That is its strength. You can try to take it to depend as well on the seeming truths at the bottom of morality.

So you have a recommendation as to a worked-out morality. Also the proposition, among others, that we cannot escape natural morality. We cannot escape the next question either. It is whether a world of bad lives exists because we have done wrong.

3
Did we wrong them?
Do we wrong them?

Political realism

Thinking about our own actions past and present is often made easier and not much good by sliding away from the grim facts that raise the question. It is made easier by avoiding the enormity of the facts, the numbers. It is also made easier by taking humanity out of the numbers, losing sight of the people, each as real as that nice girl who brings the paper to Fountain House before school, or the small daughter of our Chancellor of the Exchequer who was in the paper during her brief life.

Let us try to keep the world of bad lives in view. They include lives cut short – half-lives, lives of lost children, quarter-lives – one particular group of which could have been longer by a total of 20 million years. The bad lives also include lives devoid of physical well-being, so weak as to be not much better than nothing, and lives such as those of a people degraded in their own land by the rapacity of another people. Also lives otherwise denigrated and made self-denigrating, and lives so thin in everything as again to be only a little better than being missing. This is unlikely to be the best possible world. Leibniz, having arrived at that conclusion by reflecting on the moral perfection of the Creator, should have tested it somewhere else than in his rooms with the Dukes of Hanover.

Some say or half-say that the question of whether this world of unfortunate innocents is the result of our having done wrong does not arise. There is no real question of our moral relation to these bad lives. These realists, as they take themselves to be, cannot mean that we cannot ask the question. Plainly we can. We have. What they must mean, rather, is that it is not a sensible question, not grown-up, that people of sense or of a knowing or worldly kind do not ask it.

They may say that how a society feels about and runs its own internal life is one thing, something natural and also the subject of worked-out social moralities. How it runs its external relations, to other societies and groups of people in them, is another very different thing. They may say that all countries run their relations with other countries not primarily on the basis of morality but primarily on the basis of national self-interest. They say it is *political realism* both to see this and to engage in it.

They say or imply that all societies, when they are dealing with other societies, go beyond the sort of self-interest involved in their own social morality to an uncollaborative self-interest that is outside of morality. Or rather, in the international world, societies cannot safely advance much towards collaborative self-interest from primitive, go-it-alone or unilateral self-interest. They help arrange for their corporations to pay as little as possible for what they buy from other countries, however poor the countries, and to get paid as much as possible for what they sell. In politics they engage to some large extent in *realpolitik*, the cynical practicality of Bismarck, Germany's nineteenth-century iron chancellor, or even *machtpolitik* or power politics, which attends only to the power, if any, of nations, classes, groups or whatever, and not to needs, rights and the like.

Usually the point of our leaders taking or half-taking this view of the world is a preface to conveying that our leaders will have to run their own country's relations in some respect in this way. President Bush the younger took this line openly in going back on a major international agreement. That was the agreement to limit the emission of greenhouse gases that already have had grim effects and look like having catastrophic ones in the future.

It needs to be kept in mind here that the international relations of our societies could not consist only in political realism or national self-interest. We must remember that our leaders, as well as engaging in announcements of uncollaborative self-interest, are all the time engaging in moral judgement on other countries, certainly not always diplomatic. Our newspapers are full of it, sometimes in their editorials and opinion pieces. Do remember condemnation of the Evil Empire, a.k.a. the Soviet Union, and of course condemnations of societies said to harbour terrorists. Much of it is sincere even if statesmen are politicians – it is not just a hypocrisy that is part of political realism. It is moral judgement that licenses moral judgement in return.

Also, with respect to international morality, claims for reparation and compensation on account of past actions have been and are made. My New Labour government when it began was to have an ethical foreign policy. There have been armed interventions with good principle and feeling in them. Governments do make contributions to famine relief and help out with other disasters. If the UN Declaration of Human Rights is embarrassing and not much heard of, the United Nations does still function despite the hegemony of the United States. My Mr Blair and others speak of their moral visions. Mr Bush had one once. To the credit of Americans, the question of their own standing arose among many of them after September 11.

So it is no good trying to pretend that the question of our relation to the bad lives arises only among philosophers and vicars. But that is not all. It is not as if political realism in itself is an escape from anything like morality, the whole neighbourhood. There is a way in which our countries when they engage in political realism *are* engaged in something like morality.

To have this policy of political realism is of course to have it as a reason for actions and policies. In the case of President Bush, the reason is that something is good or profitable for Americans, or anyway some Americans. Even if this self-interest is not explicitly given as a reason by an unusually innocent president, it will be plain enough to see. But then the government of another country can feel more permitted to do the same – it can take the line that in consistency it can more vigorously or singlemindedly pursue *its* noncollaborative self-interest. This government can feel licensed and therefore go further in *realpolitik* or *machtpolitik*.

Not only the government. Entirely self-appointed representatives or agents of another country can do this. They can follow suit. They may take themselves to be doing so by flying airplanes full of ordinary people into skyscrapers. The first country's leaders will with good reason say that this is not at all consistent with their past military adventures and their support for counter-revolutionaries, let alone their position on the greenhouse gases or whatever. There are further considerations and distinctions. It is always possible to say so, sometimes conclusively. There are differences between wars or financing counter-revolutionaries and engaging in terrorism.

In short, it is not true that only moral philosophers and the like engage in such questions as that of whether we in our societies have done wrong. Politicians and journalists do it. It is pretty inescapable, as you have already heard. And there is an engagement in a side of morality in the very practice of political realism, with the usual consequent dangers. Others can perceive your reasons and use or misuse them.

A morality of relationship

There is a need to have a starting-point in the project of looking at the question of whether we have done wrong and continue to do so with respect to the bad lives. To judge something wrong or right is to judge it thus from a point of view, in fact some kind of morality. Things are clearest when you start from a worked-out morality. We have looked at a few, but there are others.

Among them are *moralities of relationship*, most heard of in connection with private lives. They have to do with special obligations a person may have because of special relationships with some other persons. Such relationships have as their paradigm the connection of a mother with her child. Other private relationships are to a loyal friend or a benefactor or someone who has been in one's life for a long time. Some say a society or country rightly engages in or ought to engage in a morality of relationship. This worked-out morality is not limited to how things are to be arranged within the boundary of a society.

Moralities of relationship in general are contrasted with what are now usually called *consequentialist moralities*. These latter are sometimes said to have to do only with the consequences or effects of actions – they judge that actions are right on the basis of their consequences or effects. Not their actual consequences, which can be entirely unexpected bad ones, or of course all their consequences right up to the end of time, but their reasonably expected consequences. The morality of humanity is of this kind, despite attending to relationships, and arguably so is the liberalism of Professor Rawls. Its principles too make rightness a matter of consequences. A morality of relationship is supposed to be radically different.

One more large complication. It is not only such a morality of relationship that is taken to be different from and opposed to consequentialism. It is one of a larger number of what can be called *moralities of special obligation*. They get strength from each other.

Some of these moralities take an action to be right if it was in accord with a particular kind of moral rule, principle, categorical imperative, law, or right. Other moralities of special obligation have it that an action can be made right by the fact that it accords with a person's autonomy or integrity, or its deriving from moral perception or intuition with respect to a situation, not from calculating consequences. Other moralities contrasted with consequentialism find an action's rightness in its being done out of a virtue or a good intention on the part of the acting person, or out of what the great eighteenth-century German philosopher Immanuel Kant described as *a pure good will*.

In all these moralities put in opposition to consequentialism, all the moralities of special obligation, we are sometimes asked to understand that the rightness of an action does not have to do with the probable consequences of the action. That is the general distinction between moralities of special obligation and consequentialism. The reason for a woman's care for a particular child is that it is her child, which fact is not a consequence of her care. Nor is it an effect of an action that it is according to a kind of moral law that is said to have nothing whatever to do with consequences or has a source in a pure good will. The moralities of special obligation are likely to have an absolute character, or at least a highmindedness. They avoid the grubbiness of adding-up – counting benefits or heads.

Our subject is a particular morality of relationship. The other non-consequentialist moralities have been mentioned, however, not just to give a better sense of a morality of relationship by noting the species and the genus of which it is a member. A morality of relationship can have added to it some or conceivably all of the other non-consequentialist moralities. Thus it can be said, for example, that an action is right because of a relationship of the acting person, along with the action's being in accord with a right or rights, and also its preserving the integrity of the person.

The particular morality of relationship that is now relevant and may be the core of such a bundle is basically one idea. It is that a society or state acts rightly when its action is in accord with its concern for its own people, or primarily in accord with that concern. The individuals who are its government do right when they act in this way, and something the same is true of every member of the society.

A general distinction, and a mystery

Questions arise about this, as about all moralities of relationship and indeed all moralities of special obligation.

Is it not a little too highminded to maintain that the moralities of relationship do not have to do with the probable consequences of actions – do not have to do with the probable consequences at all? Take the woman who makes the life of one child better when she could instead improve the life of a less fortunate child. Is it not strange to suppose, when she gives as her reason that one of them is her child, that her reason does not have to do with the probable consequences of her action? Is it really not part of the effect of a woman's action with the supermarket food that what is fed is her child? You can have second thoughts about that.

Or take a politician who says the society's resources should be used to improve the circumstances of poor Americans, or to reduce the tax burden on other Americans, or the oil or energy corporations, and not be used to do good in distant places? Is it not strange to say he may not be giving the expected consequences of his policy as his reason for it? Some hair-splitting can be engaged in with respect to what is and is not a consequence or an effect, but to much avail?

If a morality of relationship cannot arguably be understood as not having to do with the consequences of actions at all, can it be understood as not having to do *only* with the consequences of actions? As having to do with *more* than the consequences of actions? That sounds better. At any rate, what we have is the position that actions are made rightly partly by their consequences and partly by the relationship of the person doing the acting to the persons who are affected. By way of example, the Canadian government's spending on welfare at home, on international aid, and whatever else, may be made right not only by its good consequences but also by its attention to the claims of its own people.

To pause for a minute or two before thinking about that, notice that we have already upset the general distinction made between moralities of relationship and other moralities of special obligation on the one hand, and, on the other hand, moralities that locate the rightness of actions in their consequences. The distinction between so called non-consequentialism and consequentialism has been upset by the brute fact that moralities of relationship, at least, *do* have something to do with consequences.

That is not all. Contemplate what are talked of as plainly consequentialist moralities. Take a simple egalitarianism, like the one that the Hutterite people in Western Canada used to follow. It is the principle that all are to have equal lives, maybe more or less equal income over a lifetime, or more or less equal amounts of the great goods. What the egalitarianian administrators would do in our societies, if ever we put them in place, would be to look at my past life and then arrange my future in such a way as to make my life, in the end, equal to yours. If I'd had a bad start, unlike you, I would in the future get more income than you or more means to the great goods.

So do the reasons for the rightness of actions in this egalitarian morality have to do only with the probable consequences of actions? Seemingly not. They seem to have to do with my *past*. You can have much the same thought about another so-called consequentialist morality, nothing other than the morality of humanity as we have understood it. Certainly it will be offering compensations for past deprivations.

For these reasons, the general distinction between non-consequentialist and consequentialist moralities surely has to be replaced by something else. Certainly there is *some* difference between kinds of moralities. It could be that the two kinds we have should be understood differently, not in terms of consequences or non-consequences. It could be that we need to find new kinds, draw the line differently between two or more new kinds. The new difference when rightly seen may give some kind of support to conclusions that can be drawn with respect to our current subject matter.

For now, let us return to that subject matter. In particular, what is to be said of the view that an action may be made right not only by its good consequences but also by something else – the relationship of the acting person to the persons affected?

Will you agree with me, maybe on reflection, that it is a little hard to see what the reasons actually are that have to do with the relationship? Do remember that these reasons of rightness definitely are not consequences or effects of the action. Those are separate. What are these other different things? What do they have to do with? Are they facts of A's relation to B that are independent of whatever it is that A does with respect to B? How can those make a difference in rightness to what A does? Are they qualities of intentions-in-themselves? Do you have to have special moral vision to see them? Special moral sensitivity to feel them? There seems to be a mystery here.

It deepens when you have a certain thought about the morality of humanity in particular and so-called consequentialism in general. No morality will really get our attention if it supposes there is no reason for a mother favouring her child to some extent against other children. That human fact, a fact of rightness, will defeat anything that attempts to discard it. But, despite some utterances to the contrary by its critics, no half-thought-out consequentialism has ever done so. The benighted Utilitarians, beyond a doubt, whatever they might have to say of crazy examples, accepted that in general a mother's special concern for her child is a great means to the greatest happiness of the greatest number. They might have and probably did speak of the division of moral labour. You look after that one, I look after this one.

Certainly this sort of thing is true of the morality of humanity we have considered. It does not crazily suppose for a moment that the principle of saving people from bad lives by certain effective policies includes the policy of separating children from their mother. The Greek philosopher Plato, venerated by many opponents of the morality of humanity, and indeed for his attention to the virtues, did in fact have some idea about having rearing-pens for a society's children. As I am pleased to say again, this is no part of the morality we are considering. Certainly it puts a limit, a real limit, on how far parents are to go in favouring their children, but as certainly it does not include the proposition that they are to go nowhere.

So there seems to be a mystery about the special reasons we are to consider that have to do with a relationship. And it deepens, does it not, when we reflect or reflect again that these reasons are *not* the plain reasons just considered having to do with good consequences? Certainly there is no question of the special reasons in a morality of relationship being such. The philosophers of relationship are not disguised or confused Utilitarians or humanitarians. They will in fact resist our taking them as anything of the sort in the way just noticed, since to be in that position is to be on a slippery slope they do not fancy – to such a destination as our morality of fellow-feeling.

For myself, I cannot quite see that there actually are moral reasons for action of the kind we are trying to find. There even seems to me to be a kind of proof that they do not exist at all. It is as follows.

To give a reason for an action, at bottom, is to say that it will or would satisfy some desire. That is what a reason for an action is – as, incidentally, is agreed by pretty well all of my fellow-workers in that thriving part of philosophy that is the Philosophy of Mind. If something does or would satisfy no desire, it is not a reason for acting at all. To give a reason for an action *is* to present the thing as desirable – such as to satisfy some desire or other. It might be only the desire that the right thing be done. But then to give a reason for an action is necessarily to recommend it on the basis of certain effects or consequences. To come to one conclusion, saying something about an action that brought in none of its consequences just could not be a reason for an action at all.

What are we to say, then, of moralities of relationship? Well, even if they can't have in them reasons of the sort supposed, they *do* clearly have reasons in them, don't they? 'He's my son' *is* a reason for what I do. It is a reason that has to do with consequences of what I do, and it favours him, my son.

Therefore, to come to a crux, it is hard to avoid the idea that there is a strain of selfishness in the moralities of special obligation, most plainly in the moralities of relationship. Like so much of human life, they can involve a mixture of motivations, but the main one of these is looking out for yourself and people you identify with, people whose desires you share. This self-interest is different from the collaborative self-interest of ordinary morality.

Come back now to the particular morality of relationship that has to do with international relations. That is the morality that has at its core the proposition that a society or state acts rightly when its actions or policies serve the interests of its own people, or primarily serve those interests. Given our reflections on moralities of relationship generally, something seems clear. It is that there is no great difference between what we began with, political realism, and the morality of relationship that has as its principle that a government or society acts rightly when its policies and actions serve the interests of its own people. The morality of relationship boils down to a kind of selfishness.

One footnote. As we saw earlier, you cannot distinguish between two groups of moralities by saying that moralities of special obligation do not attend at all to the consequences of actions, and consequentialists attend only to consequences. Both groups of moralities concern consequences of actions in terms of things we all want, the great goods. So what shall we say here in order to get things into view, organize them?

We should draw a new line, just a little different. If you put aside Utilitarianism, and the unhappy fact that it would justify having a society with some slaves in it if the alternative was a society of less total happiness, all the remaining so-called consequentialist moralities have different kinds and degrees of concern with people at the bottom of the pile – support them in their desires for the great goods, support them in their frustration. They are *moralities of concern*.

The non-consequentialist moralities so called, by contrast, have in them a distinguishing strain of selfishness or at least self-indulgence. This is so with the one of them that is our main subject, a particular morality of relationship. Selfishness in a morality does not recommend itself. It also makes a morality less safe than it used to be. You can be viciously attacked.

Do you say, critical reader, that things are not so crystal-clear as they might be? Do you remember that ordinary morality in a society, the fact and practice of morality, was said to be partly a matter of collaborative self-interest? And that political realism was go-it-alone or unilateral self-interest? Do you add that moralities of special obligation, above all moralities of relationship, and one in particular, have now been judged as selfish? And that it has just been remarked that there is no great difference between the particular morality of relationship and the previous amorality of political realism?

I plead guilty in a way. What you have heard is not so crystal-clear as it might be if the world were simple, and in particular if morality and our motivations were simple. Attitudes, even if they have truth in them, are not as definite as rabbits. They blur into one another. You will have to put up with the fact that in the reality that is our subject-matter, there are differences of degree rather than kind. Things are not as presidents and prime ministers, and no doubt sheikhs and mullahs, prefer for their speeches and their visions.

Did we wrong them? Do we wrong them?

Libertarianism, liberalism, humanity again

Our current question is our moral relation to the bad lives in other places – the enormous numbers of lives cut short, weak, degraded, respectless and thin. Political realism is no satisfactory response, and a morality of relationship does not give us a decent answer to the question. What of the three worked-out social moralities looked at earlier? You have heard my thoughts and feelings about them, but none of them was *proved* right or wrong. Maybe supporters of the first two of them would like more attention in connection with our current question. Let us glance at them again.

According to the morality of libertarianism, what is our relation to the bad lives? It is that we have in the past had no obligation at all, no hint of one, to do anything whatever with respect to them. We have no obligation now. We might in consistency have done more to encourage the societies in question in the direction of the liberty of the basketball player and free enterprise and the multinationals – a charter for buying and selling and keeping everything for your own children. There was no need for us to do anything else.

What we have here is not so much a question of what follows from libertarianism about our moral relation to all the starvation, disease, rapine, dehumanizing and emptiness. It is more a question of what follows about libertarianism from what it takes to be our moral relation to the starvation, disease, rapine, dehumanizing and emptiness. Our relation, to repeat, is taken by libertarianism to raise or involve no question at all about our moral self-respect, our moral composure in thinking of the bad lives when we do. In simply excluding this question, however it is to be answered, the morality in question does a little more to discard itself.

Libertarianism and its tradition may be worth thinking of again, however, in connection with a further question, that of what we are to do about terrorism against us and about preventing it. Contained in this question is the prior one of the actual explanation of the occurrence of this terrorism – as distinct from any question of its justification, excuse or half-excuse. No doubt Professor Nozick's *Anarchy, State and Utopia* has not been widely read in the refugee camps in Palestine or at food camps in Africa. But it will have had some readers, and there will be more people there with a sense of what it has helped out with, the single idea of buying and selling and looking after one's own. The time has come not to pass over such a cautionary utterance, but to think about it.

To leave libertarianism for the social morality of liberalism, what has been our relation to the bad lives according to it? Presumably, in consistency, we should have been at least as active as we were in leading other societies in the direction of liberalism. Presumably we should have tried harder to secure that everybody in Malawi had the benefit of hearing about the contract argument and being in a just society. The trouble about this comes when you take your thinking off automatic pilot, where liberalism names a flight path, and remember that it is not at all clear what the direction actually is.

Evidently this liberalism has a source in some concern wider than that of libertarianism, a concern for something more than private property and its holders. To linger for a moment, Professor Rawls remarks that his idea of a just society is a special case of a more general idea: 'All social values – liberty and equality, income and wealth, and the bases of self-respect – are to be distributed equally unless an unequal distribution of any, or all, of these values is to everyone's advantage.'

It sounds OK, better than OK. He rightly says, though, that it is vague and requires interpretation – which to my mind, despite a great deal of philosophical prose, it never really gets. What liberalism deems to be necessary in terms of inequality is left obscure, and that is just one mystery. As a consequence, what it is to be taken as suggesting about our past and present relation, our moral relation, to those other people who die early and so on, is also left obscure. If you don't know what a morality comes to, if you don't know whether it is just a philosophical celebration of America, you don't know what it says you ought to have been doing.

It cannot be said that liberalism is like libertarianism in allowing no question to arise of our moral relation to bad lives. It is not vicious. Some of the feeling in liberalism, an impulse in it, is a generosity. But it remains uncertain what, in terms of it, we are to

70

think of our past and present with respect to the bad lives. It is possible to think of it, in fact, as a morality of bad conscience. But that remains indefinite, no very clear conclusion. It does not give me satisfaction to add one other thought. Suspicion has attached to inexplicitness about things in every part of the whole history of human life, including trials and official inquiries. Does liberalism conceal too much self-interest?

Nor, to be cautionary again, will we have made friends with the students in Pakistan and Mozambique by being identified, to the extent that we are, with a social morality left undefined. The question of whether we have wronged their people will not be contemplated by the students in terms of an elusive morality. They will not be very ready to look at questions in terms of a morality that is reminiscent of a religion that requires or advocates belief as a means to and before understanding. Leaping before looking. The students will ask for understanding first.

You will not be surprised that I myself will proceed with our question in terms of the morality of humanity. Given a commitment to it, have we wronged those who have had the bad lives and those who have them now? In terms of the principle that we need to save people from bad lives by certain effective policies, do we bear a guilt? Do we bear a guilt that will be of relevance to judgements on the killers of September 11?

You need not be convinced, of course, that I am asking the only right question, proceeding in terms of the only correct morality. If we could only learn from following our guides, and not by doubting our guides, we could not learn much. Conceivably you will see what is right by seeing what is wrong.

You know much of my reason for proceeding in terms of the morality of humanity. What it comes to in good part is the short-comings of the two alternatives. As you will gather, it is my idea that related shortcomings are to be found in other social moralities that have affected our societies less, including a soup of doctrine called communitarianism, a response to liberalism on which it is not absolutely necessary to lift the lid. Another reason for proceeding in terms of the morality of humanity is that it can be argued to be in better accord – no more than *better* accord – with the natural fact and practice of morality.

That is, it can seem to fit better not only with the fact of our sympathy for persons not closely related to us, but also with the facts of self-interest and of our having reasons that others can take over. It is posssible to be as much impressed, somehow, by the fact and practice of morality as by any attempt to put it into explicit principles. It is possible, therefore, to be more confident of a principle that is closer to its nature. That closeness, by the way, may be shared with certain religious moralities – complicated though they are by inconsistency, the metaphysics of belief in God, and also the worldly institution of religion. In particular some Catholic morality in South America comes to mind.

So it is by way of the principle of humanity that we will look at the bad lives. Or rather we will use it to look at the bad lives conceived in a certain way, our own main way. This is in terms of certain causes of them rather than others. In a sentence, we have mainly had in mind bad lives owed to causes other than violence – causes other than war of several kinds, terrorism of several kinds, attacks and counter-attacks, and so on. We have mainly had in mind bad lives owed to the ordinary and more or less peaceful conduct of relations between people and between peoples. These relations are most importantly economic.

As already remarked (pp. 11, 24), this is a concentration on the ongoing circumstances of life on our earth rather than on what is less pervasive and constant, the violence. It is a concentration, so to speak, on the baseline of our activities in all places and recent times, and especially with African, Islamic and other poorer societies. It is a concentration on what has not stopped, and, you may therefore think, is yet more involved in the bad lives than our violence.

To put the matter differently again, we mainly have been and will be concerned with bad lives that bring to mind the possibility of violations of the first three rather than the fourth policy of the principle of humanity (p. 54). The first three had to do with increasing and transferring ordinary means to well-being, the fourth with non-violence.

Did we wrong them? Do we wrong them?

This is not to diminish the other subject-matter – bad lives owed to wars, proxy-wars, terrorism and what is called state-terrorism, and so on. Who or what *could* diminish it? To those who have kept themselves half-informed, and half-independent of our media, of what purports to be just information, even all the information, what is needed by way of reminder is only some names: Palestine, Nicaragua, Indonesia, Turkey, Columbia, and Iraq since the Kuwait war was over. This violence, as we know, is the subject of charges against us by great moral judges, above all their charges of vicious inconsistency. It has not been my idea to take away from these judgements, but to turn to a subject at least as large, and one where it may be yet more possible to reach conclusions. That table of statistics is not disputable at all – it is not already a matter of confusions, political salesmanship, public relations in place of open truth, less rather than more intelligence, propaganda and ideology, and sometimes lies.

Acts and omissions

You may think that really we have got to the end of our question already. That to embrace the morality of humanity in order to answer the question is already to condemn ourselves with respect to the bad lives we have in mind. That just to contemplate this morality as the test is already to contemplate condemnation. In fact, that is not so. It is not so since a large question can be taken to arise about this morality. It can be taken to arise particularly when it is thought of, naturally enough, in terms not of one society but in terms of relations between societies – or between an alliance of people across different societies on the one hand, and, on the other hand, other people across those societies, maybe the poor.

The principle, again, is that we need to *save* people from bad lives by the policy, in particular, of transferring means to well-being, means to the great goods, from the better-off to the badly-off. Anything else is wrong. That principle, on an ordinary understanding, rides over something which almost all of us live by, a distinction between acts and omissions, in view a moment ago.

We take it that to *omit* to do something, with a certain effect, may not be wrong even if *acting* with that effect or something like it would be wrong. There is a difference between letting die and killing, much used in medical ethics. There is a difference between a doctor just letting the patient's pneumonia take its course and his giving the patient a fatal injection. He may get into bad trouble for the second.

There is a difference too, we assume, between not donating to Oxfam or the Red Cross for famine relief and doing something else. That would be a leader's ordering his armed forces to stop the food convoys getting through to starving people for a while, maybe with an idea, unspoken and unspeakable, of putting indirect or moral or political pressure on the other side. We take it there would be a difference between not donating for famine relief and giving the order, even if the effect in the two cases would be much the same. The difference is not something we're sure about, but it informs much of our lives, and plays a large part in ordinary morality.

Is there a difference of fact between what we call acts and omissions? More important, *is* there a difference such that the omissions are not wrong, or not so wrong as the related acts are or would be?

Well, take my action today of paying $1,200 for the air fares to Venice, giving my credit card number on the phone to the travel agent. That was an ordinary action with an ordinary effect, getting the seats. In doing the thing, I omitted to contribute $1,200 to Oxfam. If I'd done that instead, some lives would have been saved.

What exactly was the omission – what exactly was my *not contributing the $1,200 to Oxfam*? Was the omission just the ordinary action of paying the money for the Venice fares identical with it? You can say so, but you get into problems. One is that it seems you will have to say that paying the $1,200 for the fares was *also* my not buying a certain piece of furniture. Since not contributing to Oxfam is different from not buying the piece of furniture, they can't *both* be my single ordinary action of paying $1,200 for the fares.

It seems better to say that an omission consists not in exactly an ordinary action but in an action's not being another one. Or in a run of actions not including a certain one. My failing to switch on the burglar alarm at 10 p.m. was the fact that what I was then doing was not a switching-on of the alarm. My not writing to my sister today wasn't identical with a run of actions, but was the fact that they didn't include writing to her. You can ask, of course, what this thing is – an action not being another one, or a run of actions not including a certain one. You can get befuddled about that, as I have myself before now. We can leave the metaphysics to somebody else.

Some things, the only relevant things, do seem dead clear. My not doing something is up to me, and it has effects. There are those two facts about it. Because of them, people sometimes get put in jail. Or take an example from that scene in the street last night when you gave up your wallet and the guy *didn't* pull the trigger. His not pulling the trigger was up to him, his doing, and it had an effect – your being alive today. That effect is as real as any other effect of his not pulling the trigger – say a certain bullet's still being right there in his gun today.

So there might be some kind of difference between an ordinary action and an omission, but not one that is any use to us if we want to feel better about our lives. My not giving the $1,200 to Oxfam, which definitely is something I do, and something bound up with giving it to the airline, has the effect of some lives being lost, the same effect as the possible action of ordering your armed forces to stop the food convoys getting through for a while.

Are you getting a bit huffy because you don't like this proposition about the effects of your life, maybe because of where it could lead, and you don't see how to reject it? You are in for some more of that feeling. If you don't like the prospect, shut the book, or sell it, or tear out the pages one by one and dispose of them in a suitable way. You can do that. But there's something else that none of us can do.

We can't deal well with things of importance by saying that some stuff is philosophy, or just philosophy. In fact this philosophy, all philosophy when it's worth it, is the effort of trying to get things straight, seeing when there is no distinction, making distinctions when they're necessary. It's that kind of logic. The sort of thing you are rightly calling philosophy is already in and needs to get into more of life. It needs to get into your thinking if you want to think well about the matters of importance, like 3,000 killings on September 11. You can be sure, too, as already mentioned, that other people are thinking about these matters, maybe not well. Some of them could act again on what you're not thinking about.

What we have got so far is that my giving my card number on the phone to the travel agent involved two real effects. We got the seats, and some lives were lost. Giving my card number therefore involved an effect like the effect of a possible act of ordering your men not to let the food convoys through for a while in order to put political pressure on your enemy.

The general problem is that an awful lot of what we do, in America, Britain and so on, consists in actions that involve omissions – they involve an effect something like the effect of an imaginable or actual act, and the act would be or is wrong, maybe monstrous. We want to think there is a moral difference between our omissions and such acts, resting on some difference of fact, but it is not clear what it could be.

As already implied by the example of the man in the street with the gun, by the way, the difference of fact of course can't be that a 'not' turns up in the name or description of some activity of mine taken as an omission. For a small start, the related act you imagine, a killing, can also be described negatively, as 'not letting somebody live'.

Causes and conditions

Here is a hopeful thought that seems to go against what we have just concluded about effects. The couple of deaths that would take place if I were actually to act, actually do a killing or give the order to stop the food getting through, would be the result of what it is natural to call my personal activity. The couple of deaths, if I pay out money for the flights to Venice, would not be.

To make that thought a bit more precise, the couple of deaths in the first case would definitely be *caused* by me. But, whatever we say about effects, it's not at all clear that I am *the cause* of the couple of deaths when I pay for the Venice tickets. I am not what earlier was called the human cause, or the cause in any other sense. Weren't those famine deaths *caused*, rather, by conditions that I and a lot of other people didn't change? There has to be *some* truth in this, but what is it? Is it really a truth about causation? Some truth not noticed when we allowed that act and omission can have similar effects? And some truth that makes a moral difference?

What is a cause, generally speaking? It is one thing in a set of things that makes something else happen, guarantees it. That match just lit, and the cause was that you struck it. Of course other facts were part of the story – for a start, there had to be oxygen in here. We can call the oxygen one of the conditions. Think about this pair of things, the striking and the oxygen. Each of them was required or necessary for the lighting. Each of them, also, if everything else was already on hand, made it certain the match would light. They are exactly on a par there too. What we call a cause and what we call a standing condition are exactly the same with respect to the main relations between an effect and what precedes it.

That subtracts one hope of a difference between an omission and an act. It isn't true that an omission is less important causally than some other thing in the set of conditions for the effect – the one we call the cause. A standing condition is exactly as necessary and neces-sitating with respect to an effect as whatever we call the cause. But, you say, even if they are exactly as necessary and necessitating, there *is* some difference between them – one is still the cause and the other isn't. OK.

When you ask *why* we call one thing the cause and another not, though, you run into a lot of hopeful answers. One answer is that if you take the set of conditions for an effect, the cause is always the human action – for example striking the match rather than the oxygen being present. But we pick out causes where there aren't any actions at all – say where the effect is an earthquake. Nor is it true that the cause is always a change in a thing, as some people think, or an abnormal event, or the last event before the effect. Or some unknown thing that results in the effect when that unknown thing comes together with other known conditions. That is the case with what we call the cause of cancer. There are counter-examples you can work out to all these hopeful ideas.

To cut a long story short, the cause of some effect is the preceding condition that interests us, or that it is in our interest or to our advantage to concentrate on. It serves some purpose of ours to focus on it. And so, to go back to where we were, we can say if we want that giving my card number to the travel agent for the tickets was not the cause of a couple of people being dead from famine, but killing a couple of people or giving the order to stop the food trucks would be the cause of their being dead. That is certainly a difference.

The trouble is that it is no difference of the kind we are after, as you can easily come to see. If killing them would be wrong, and the omission would have the same effect, just as much so, then surely the omission remains just as wrong even if we are not *interested* in the omission and are *interested* in something else in the same circumstance for the couple of deaths. That's inevitable, isn't it? What does it matter if my omission just counts as a condition, not a cause? I could have changed this condition having to do with me. I can also get interested in it.

Isn't the same true – the omission remains as wrong – if it serves some interest or purpose or desire of ours to concentrate on something other than the omission? A murder doesn't become right because it's really in my interest. Certainly it doesn't follow from the fact that something is good for me, or good for a majority, or good for Americans, or rather some Americans, that it is right.

Good intentions

A different and large thought about acts and omissions has to do with intentions in them or from which they come. You can think of such intentions as desiring or desirous thoughts that picture or represent the action. They either do that in advance, maybe the day before, or at the time of acting. Typically they are very different in the acts and omissions we consider. Think again about somebody's giving their card number for holiday flights. In particular, think of it in terms of what it involves, the omission to make a donation to Oxfam or the Red Cross.

This omission can be unintentional, and it can be what we can call half-intentional, and it could conceivably be fully intentional. These possibilities can be defined quickly.

Did we wrong them? Do we wrong them?

Somebody *half-intentionally* omits to do something, like not contribute to Oxfam by giving their card number for the holiday flights, when they don't then think of contributing – don't picture the action as the omission – but they did in their earlier life think of contributing and then consciously fall into the habit of not contributing. The idea of giving money came to mind from time to time, they thought about it, and they didn't do anything positive. And so, when they book the holiday tickets, they don't think of the omission, have that intention.

To say quickly what it is for an omission to be *unintentional*, one of these hasn't been preceded, in the person's life, by any thought of not omitting the thing. This is the case of anybody who has never heard of Oxfam or the like. It is also the case of somebody who has heard the name, but for whatever reason hasn't had a real thought of contributing. It's not something that happens at all in his kind of life. There is also the bare possibility about the omission that it could be *fully intentional*. This would be the bizarre case where the person gives his card number and his intention pictures this in terms of the omission, maybe pictures it with the effect of a couple of deaths.

This sketch of three categories of intentions could be replaced by something a lot better, more psychologically realistic, and longer. Such a description would be of a range or spectrum of cases of intentionality, many of them shading into one another, or maybe a number of ranges or spectrums of cases. They would have to do with kinds and degrees of knowledge and feeling, with sorts of remembering, willing, deliberateness and carelessness. They would throw light on the pretty good but unsimple connection of omissions with non-violent ways of proceeding and of acts with force or violence. But without taking the time to replace the three-part sketch with something better we can get to the main points here about differences between acts and omissions.

One point is that the acts we have in mind, say the killings, are fully intentional or something close, but the omissions that most of us have in mind are something like unintentional or half-intentional. That makes a large difference in our thinking between the acts and the omissions. It is a difference that affects how we feel about the agents, above all about the contemplated killers. It is a difference that connects closely with our thoughts about kinds and degrees of responsibility.

A second and related point is that the intentions in the case of the killings – what is intended – would be monstrous or evil. Whatever more is to be said of someone who omits to contribute to Oxfam, it is not that we take them to be monstrous or evil. In fact we may take them to be doing something creditable rather than just going on a holiday. Maybe saving money for university. We think well of the omitters, then, or anyway not badly.

That is fine, but these two points leave another one standing. It is the main point. It is not hard to get to.

The question before us has been and is about whether certain things were and are wrong. It is a question that is clear enough. Expressed differently, it is the question of whether things ought not to have been done, and ought not to be done now. It is plain to almost all of us that the question of the wrongness of an action or the like is different from the question of what is to be said about the person with respect to the particular action. We all know I can out of blameless ignorance do the wrong thing. I can do the wrong thing out of the highest or good or tolerable intentions. More generally, I can do the wrong thing and for good reason not be held fully morally responsible for it, or responsible at all. I can also do the wrong thing and not be a terrible or monstrous person (pp. 7, 9).

The main point is that our omissions can be wrong even if we have something less than a full degree of responsibility for them and even if they come from tolerable or better intentions. They can be wrong even if we, or many or some of us, cannot be held fully responsible for them. It must be added that in seeing this we also come upon an explanation of why we are all inclined to take the possible actions in question as wrong and our actual omissions as otherwise. It is that we run together the question of actions being right or wrong with the other questions of responsibility and general moral standing.

It has to be admitted there is room for confusion. In the first place, there *are* connections between right actions and good intentions. The

Did we wrong them? Do we wrong them?

right thing is often enough done from a perfect intention. Also, right actions can be defined or spoken of in terms of an intention – as actions that would be done out of a certain intention. The morality of humanity or fellow-feeling, that account of right actions, can be defined secondarily as the morality that requires that all of us are to try to act with certain intentions – those that would be had by the best and best-informed judges with the aim of saving people from bad lives by certain policies. Plainly enough, right actions can also be defined or spoken of in terms of a kind of person.

None of that affects the general point that we can do the wrong thing and earn little or no moral disapproval for the action, and without being low-grade persons. Above all, it does not follow from our ordinary intentions and characters that we are not doing the wrong thing. In particular, it does not follow from our ordinary intentions and characters that we are not doing the wrong thing in our omissions.

Another hope, and a conclusion or two

Are you inclined at this point to go back to what we put aside earlier, the moralities of special obligation? Do you want to dig in your heels and say, in particular, that somehow it just *is* the good intention that makes an action right? Maybe, with Kant, that what makes an action right is its coming from a pure good will?

You will have to say what makes an intention a good one, of course. The immediate answer for almost everyone is that it is an intention to do an action that will have good effects. Obviously you can't follow them in that answer. This line of thought would come to nothing for you. What you wanted to do was to have an action count as right or anyway not wrong *despite* its effects. But by way of our ordinary talk of an intention you would make it count as wrong exactly because of its effects.

You may now think of a more radical line of escape. Some philosophers have, as already intimated. Here you take an action to be right or not wrong on account of the intention, and try to understand a good or bad intention entirely independently of the effects of action. It's some funny kind of intention. The idea is that it has some intrinsic property of goodness. This will not be like generosity where that is ordinarily understood, of course, in terms of actions and their effects. It will not be loyalty or whatever where that is understood in the same ordinary way. A good intention, I guess, just glows a little.

This takes us back to where we were with a morality of relationship (p. 66). In thinking of an action done out of a funny intention we are in fact thinking of an action done for some reason. We have to be. In the cases we are thinking of, what is the reason? We are told that it is no consequence of the action, that it has nothing to do with the consequence of the action. In that case it can satisfy no desire, no desire at all. But then it cannot be a reason for action. Of course *something* makes the person act in the cases we are thinking of. The only possibility, it seems, is some selfish or self-indulgent reason.

The main conclusion of all this, or the first of two main ones, is that it is hard to see that our omissions with respect to the bad lives are less wrong than the related acts. I mean our omissions with respect to the appalling numbers of lives that are bad because of starvation, disease, rapine, dehumanizing, and emptiness. This conclusion that we do wrong is grim and seemingly unavoidable.

Was it improbable in terms of the fact and practice of natural morality? No, it can be said pretty much to derive from it. The grim conclusion derives, first, from the indubitable fact that a reason for or against one action is a reason for or against a like one. It is in accord, too, with the sympathy for distant persons in natural morality. Such a conclusion has not been taken to be in our interest, but, thirdly, this has not been entirely obvious. It is somewhat less obvious since September 11. Such a conclusion, finally, accords with my sense of the plain truth in morality. Remember the man pressing the button. Also the woman (pp. 36, 37).

What the conclusion goes against is not the nature of our ordinary morality, so to speak, but its content. Its conventions and rules. It goes against the assumption that when I buy the tickets for Venice, I do nothing wrong, have no other obligation. It would not be the first time that ordinary morality was wrong. Its history is the history not only of our humanity, but also of our inhumanity.

It is hard to resist this conclusion about our ordinary actions, the conclusion that in the course of them we do as wrong as we would by bringing about bad lives by killing and the like. I stick to it. But it is worth noting that something less strong could be said instead. By itself this would be enough for now and for our further inquiry.

Most of us *do* take the right action in some situation to be the action, given the best available information and judgement, that will turn out for the best, taking everything into account. That is our general understanding of the right action (p. 7). We then go on to a further position – a definition of what it is to turn out for the best. We may define the best action in the way of the morality of humanity as the one that saves people from bad lives. But a retreat I have in mind has to do with the prior general understanding of the right action.

There can be no doubt that *this* understanding makes the rightness or wrongness of an action independent of the actual intentions in it. An action can be wrong despite coming from good or tolerable intentions. Suppose you now want to lay claim to the term 'right action', or 'action that ought to be done', or 'morally obligatory action'? Suppose you want to use these terms differently. You want to use them in such a way that an action is right if it comes from a good intention or the like. You think you can escape the problems just noticed with a morality of intentions and you want to try.

Feel free. There remains the question that so far we have expressed as the question of an action's rightness. If you walk off with the name, and some of its connotations, the question itself will not go away. It will remain fundamental. It is the question, for a start, whose answers then determine what is and what is not against the law – i.e. it gives rise to what admittedly is different from it, legal obligation and the like. More than that, it is the question closest to what concerns us most in our lives: what happens to us and others. It is the question of the way the world is to be insofar as it is within our control. Nobody, I hope, would dream of rejecting a possible world full of good effects of actions in favour of a possible world full of distress and horror but with every intention somehow good.

Time could be spent trying to qualify the conclusion we have, to put it in the same way as before, that our omissions are as wrong as certain possible acts. Time could be spent trying to qualify the particular conclusion that giving the credit card number for the tickets to Venice gets us into something about as wrong as a possible act of killing a couple of people. Time could be spent, here instead of elsewhere, in trying to set out differences between dying and being killed. It could be spent facing the complication that some dyings are worse for the person than being killed. Time could also be spent in a different way, reflecting on facts noticed earlier about the want of generosity on the part of some Africans and Arabs with respect to their own people. There were also other reassurances contemplated.

These qualifications, and reassurances, when fully set out, would still be overwhelmed by our conclusion about ourselves. The wrong we have done to those with bad lives would not be much touched by these items. Go back to them yourself if you want (pp. 14–16, 23).

Ask some other questions too if you want. Might it be that one person's omissions aren't seriously wrong because one person doing better would hardly help at all – just be a drop in an empty bucket? Can the 'ought' in 'I ought to do better' really be serious, a real 'ought'? Does the established human fact that we're not doing better actually show, somehow, that we don't have to? The German philosopher Georg Wilhelm Friedrich Hegel thought so. Is doing better just too much to ask? Again, what about looking out for our own children? Is your guide not serious, because he is only writing a book? Is he a hypocrite?

The first of three responses is that a German railwayman might have made himself more comfortable in 1943 by asking these questions after he had the thought that he ought to be doing something against the genocide of the Jews and the Gypsies and the Poles and the rest. He ought to have been doing something, however.

Also, in connection with our omissions, if you're feeling that there is moral safety in numbers, that everybody will be struck or detained by the sceptical questions about our omissions, you have forgotten a lot of people. You could start by remembering the bottom tenths of population in Malawi, Mozambique, Zambia and Sierra Leone. They will not be much struck. Are they interested parties and therefore not to be much considered? And are you not an interested party?

There is also a third response to the questions, starting with the one about one individual being of little help. What if he is one of your elected leaders, maybe with a big majority? What if he is in some position of economic power, maybe the World Bank? Or the owner of a television and newspaper corporation? You can't omit to do what you can't do, or give what you haven't got. On the other hand, some people can omit a lot. Some people are big omitters.

The conclusion that we have done wrong carries an implication having to do with responsibility, a second main conclusion. It is something that can be missed on account of facts noticed earlier. Those were that in thinking of omissions with respect to the bad lives, most of us have in mind unintentional or half-intentional omissions, omissions not at the time pictured as omissions but as something else. Further, they are of course pictured as innocent actions – such as going on a holiday. This way of thinking about our omissions helps us to avoid the truth that the actions in question are wrong.

But this ordinary way of thinking about our omissions is one thing and what we should be thinking about them is another. One thing is that it is not entirely clear what the facts are.

How many of us are really unintentional in our omissions? Some of us have never had Oxfam or whatever in our conscious worlds, but how many? Maybe a smallish minority of us. Of those of us who can be described, too simply, as half-intentional in our omissions, how many have their attention caught once again by appeals for donations? Maybe a lot. Could there be a significant number of us, including readers of thoughts like this, paragraphs like this, who omit fully intentionally? No doubt we do not picture the very deaths we are not preventing, but do have in mind that there are those other things we could be doing with our money.

What this comes to is a proposition to the effect that there is among us *a responsibility* for the bad lives. It is not just that our actions are wrong, but that there is a responsibility on our part for them. There is a truth, to return to an earlier distinction (p. 7), having to do with our being responsible for things and our rightly being held responsible for them. The truth exists, and will go on doing so in the absence of a struggle to express it more fully and explicitly.

We pass by, too, the whole complicated story of the extent to which the bad lives are owed to our very positive actions rather than our omissions, owed to our sins of commission rather than omission. I am not talking about force and violence, including war and the like, which we are also not concentrating on (p. 24). I mean, mainly, economic actions that are clear-eyed, that are something or other like fully intentional with respect to causing bad lives. Executives generally know if the chemical factories they build in other countries are dangerous.

All this turns up in the long and large subject-matter, about which something will be said later (p. 129). That is unrestrained big business, or the corporate sector or what is traditionally called capitalism, and also exploitation, protectionism until it serves its national purpose and then what is called free trade, ruinous loans, destruction of resources, cheap labour, the World Bank, the International Monetary Fund, and globalization.

There is a snapshot of it all, by the way, in your cup of coffee, not a snapshot to be disdained for its simplicity. It is that those who actually spend their lives growing our coffee get 10 per cent of what we pay for it, which leaves 10 per cent for the exporters in their country, 25 per cent for our retailers, and 55 per cent for the food corporations in the middle. There is a more grisly snapshot to do with the drug corporations maintaining profits while people are dying of AIDS.

It seems to me, certainly, that critics of our positive actions and policies of an economic kind have an overwhelming and grim case against us. If all of us are implicated, the case is against some of us in particular. It is a case that can meet much obfuscation, and needs another book, with as much claim to attention. But it is not a case that we need to consider now in order to go forward. Our omissions are a simpler case, less disputable, enough by themselves.

After September 11, according to the papers, Americans asked the question of why they are hated. They asked why there is anti-Americanism. It was as if it is a hard question, about all Americans, maybe needing an answer from a psychoanalyst, or a culture-theorist or a novelist capable of looking into the mind of Islam and diagnosing its paranoia. Some of the columnists in the papers said the cause of the hatred was envy – envy of freedom, democracy and the blessings of capitalism. We will get around to those subjects, but we do not have to do so in order to have a view of the question.

It is a pretty ignorant or dimwitted question. Americans and we who are with them, maybe with them all the way, are hated by people for the reason that what we are doing, what it comes to, is destroying them and their lives. If objections to that answer can be raised or manufactured, it is an answer that is hard to miss. Did a lot of Americans really not think of it, really have to ask the question? Did some columnists ask it for them in order to avoid the fact that it was already answered? Do many Americans think that aid for Afghanistan after the bombing, given the fact of the rest of the poor world, comes to anything much?

It is possible to think that the conclusion that we do wrong with respect to the bad lives is something most of us knew or half-knew. It is possible that the effort just put into supporting the conclusion in the previous pages is best viewed as getting us to see that we knew it. I myself am tempted to go further, in bad company. In Plato's *Republic*, Thrasymachus says that justice is no pure or high thing but just what is in the interests of the stronger, maybe the rich. It hasn't done his reputation any good. Still, it is possible to be tempted to a cynicism not only about the law but also about a lot of moral philosophy. Maybe that is why moral philosophy has never had so respectable a place in philosophy as other parts of the subject.

Allow me a last reflection on it. It is possible to think and feel, anyway in one mood, that all the stuff about moralities of relationship, and special obligations, and there really being a big difference between acts and omissions, and good intentions again, is not really serious inquiry, not really exploring into the unknown, not a justification of ourselves that many of us really begin to believe. It is just apologetics. It is doing what you can, maybe brazenly, about a bad conscience about others that cannot be doubted.

We all know, don't we, that this stuff about special obligations and what-not is not going to deal with the fact that we have actually been letting them die like flies and we still are? We could have changed it, anyway a lot, and we didn't. We could change it now, anyway a lot, and we aren't. Forget all my own philosopher's half-technical stuff about omissions too, if you want. You're left with the plain fact that we could have done otherwise and we didn't, and that this had awful effects. You can wonder if the moral philosophy about relationship and special obligations and so on is humanly necessary apologetics, a humanly necessary diversion from the facts. Still guff, though.

4

The twin towers,
and democracy

Oneness in extremity

To be on an airliner and look around and see the people and be able to stick to the plan of flying it into a skyscraper is to be hideous, and to persist if they come to know the plan is to be monstrous. Nothing can be thought that will take away from such judgements. What else can be said will not reduce them. The terms 'hideous' and 'monstrous', by their use in connection with the killers of September 11, are recalled from metaphor and loose talk to original meanings having to do with being repulsive and being inhuman.

These feelings about the killers seem in a way to be under-described as moral feelings. They have something else in them, something older.

This revulsion is not the result of the killers going back on any self-interested collaboration between people to conduct life in a certain way – it is not mainly owed to our parents having done something to keep the agreement by setting an example to us in their reactions to awfulness. Nor is this revulsion, to recall a second side of natural morality, a matter of feelings that comes from believing that the killers were selfishly inconsistent with what we or they take to be reasons for conduct or principles of conduct.

These feelings are also different from certainty derived from real truths at the bottom of morality. These were brought into view by that imagined and contrived example of the man with the button (p. 36), and are now brought into better view by the reality of September 11. Finally, this part of our response is only related to, and in a way the very opposite of, our feelings of sympathy for strangers, people at a distance from us.

This part of our response, for what the description is worth, is human identification of a primal kind with the fear and horror of those many who were about to be killed. It is an identification felt by almost everyone, perhaps not felt only by those who have been degraded by themselves or others, out of whatever supposed necessity. If this identification is related to our sympathy for others in ordinary life, strong sympathy for lives terribly dragged down or oppressed, it is different in being true empathy with others in extremity. Nothing natural stands between us in this corporeal identification, about which further theory would at best be otiose.

This oneness can perhaps be distinguished as another and fifth part of the fact of ordinary morality, a part having to do with extremity, and mainly with people being killed. It was Immanuel Kant, mentioned earlier in connection with the idea of the pure good will and moralities of special obligation, who had the misfortune to live when and where it was possible to think that morality goes entirely wrong when it has emotion in it, when it is led astray by feeling and departs from the categorical imperative to stick to impartial rules derived from something called reason. We need not follow him in his morality of special obligation. However urged to do so by revising scholars, we need not take a single step with him.

It is true, no embarrassing truth, that our human identification with the many victims of September 11 is a matter of knowing them – in the sense of knowing them to have been people like ourselves. No ignorance, distance or merely general knowledge limits this sympathy. Nor does any need for imagination limit it. We know from inside what was in the last telephone calls, about which knowledge any explanation by way of a common culture would also be otiose. After September 11 it was understandable but not necessary that this closeness should be confirmed by the biographies of ordinary lives in the newspapers. We wanted but did not need them.

Not to have the reaction of natural morality to September 11, with the special revulsion that is a matter of identification with others in extremity, is surely to be disqualified from thinking about terrorism. To anticipate lines of thought that would make the killers of September 11 less terrible would surely be to disqualify yourself from thinking about that day. It cannot be that there is nothing else to be thought about and felt. But it may be that these natural feelings about September 11 are necessities, whatever may have to be added to them.

Definitions of violence

To go forward properly from here, it will be best first to detain ourselves. There is the matter of what terrorism in general is to be taken to be. We need to settle for ourselves a dispute in which definitions of it are exchanged by academics and journalists as part of their ongoing projects, and used by politicians and other national leaders as political tools, strategies of international politics, and items of morality or pretended morality. To have a general understanding of terrorism will help with a further question about September 11 as well as with our remaining questions.

We can work down to what terrorism is, label a part of reality, by starting with *violence* in general. This we can take to be

a use of physical force that injures, damages, violates or destroys people or things.

Physical force that just changes something, however noisily or dramatically, as in the case of a machine or other process, is not violence. There has to be injury or other change for the worse, whatever good may be intended or also come about. Violence, then, before any more is said, is not only a matter of ordinary facts of change, but of disvalues we put on them or find in them.

A part of violence so conceived is *political violence*. However we finally define it, it has a further intention and end. That is political change or political continuity in the policies or the officers of a state, directed to a final end taken to justify it. This final end is that of changing a society or societies or keeping things as they are. This final end has to do with fundamental things in human and social life.

According to our earlier characterization, it has to do with the great goods, or, in our world as it is, bad lives. Who is to get what or keep what great good or what amount? Freedom and power is the great good that comes to mind first, but it is not alone in the final ends of acts or campaigns of political violence. This violence may of course be characterized otherwise than in terms of the great goods. It may be characterized in another and more passionate or accusatory style, or from within a religious or patriotic tradition, or an ethnic, ideological, anti-American, or American tradition. Those who carry out the violence, believing that it is justified by its end, may of course be absolutely wrong. They may be pursuing vicious shares of the great goods. They may be irrational, even crazy.

Political violence so far conceived, and presupposing the initial definition of violence in general, is

violence with a political and ultimately a social intention.

That evidently includes, for a start, acts and campaigns by the state within its society. It includes, that is, activity in accordance with law and the resulting decisions of the sovereign body of a state. It may include, for example, what a policeman does in this way to a rioter with a club or rubber bullets. It may include persecution of a minority.

Here and elsewhere there is room for stipulation or decision, in some accordance with ordinary usages – of course there is no simple truth to be announced, no one true definition to be discovered. We do ordinarily connect political and much other violence with illegality. So it will be natural to exclude from political violence the activities of a state and its agents in its own society so long as they are according to that society's law. This will leave open the possibility, of course, that activities by policemen, state security services and the like can count as violence if they are against the law. It will leave open the possibility, indeed the probability, that the British army's killing of Irish civil rights marchers on Bloody Sunday in Londonderry in 1972 was political violence.

Political violence as first conceived above includes war as well as such activities as those of riot police. That is, it includes armed conflict between states or societies, or a state and a would-be state, or would-be states. There is a reason, not having to do with exactly that initial idea of war, to exclude all war from political violence – and hence from the kind of political violence to which we are working our way, which is terrorism. The reason again has to do with conformity to ordinary usage. Political violence is not taken to be as large as war. War is activity of a certain magnitude, organization and persistence. Even a small war, a real war that is small, requires an army or other armed force, a large and commanded number of men fighting in unison, using the resources of a state or something like one, and it goes on for a while. Probably a war requires two such armies. An attack, even September 11, is not a war itself, even though it is natural enough to speak of it as an act of war.

If we exclude war from political violence, as we shall, we do not thereby exclude from it all smaller-scale uses of force by a state or would-be state or a society. Still, there is reason to exclude some. Again this has to do with legality. Suppose we now had what we do not have, a clear and full body of international law, at least fairly widely accepted. Suppose a state is engaging in a smaller-scale use of force against another state. Suppose, further, that this use of force, maybe truly defensive rather than an attack or counter-attack said to be self-defence, is in full accord with the body of international law. It is not natural to think of this activity as political violence. There is the same naturalness, if some uncertainty, if we think of activity in the world as it is arguably in accordance with international law as we have it.

Political violence, reconceived with these considerations about legality and war in mind, is

> violence with a political and social intention – either violence within a society that is illegal or smaller-scale violence between states or societies that is not according to international law.

This conception of political violence evidently covers what we first have in mind as our subject-matter, including the Twin Towers and so on, but it leaves various matters entirely unaffected. They will need to be kept in mind. They have to do with morality, official violence, and cat's paw violence.

Despite the presupposed definition of violence generally, as something that injures or the like, the given conception of political violence does not make it by definition wrong. It does not definitely morally condemn it. Illegality is not wrongfulness or immorality – there have been and there are morally terrible laws, corrupt bodies of law, selfish bodies of law. It serves nobody's end for long to confuse what is legal with what is right. A philosopher or two used to try, but they are not well remembered.

Nor does this conception of political violence imply that something else in the same neighbourhood that it does not cover is right. It does not imply that the legal activities of policemen and the like in societies are necessarily right. Remember Hitler's police. It does not imply that any police activities are necessarily right. It does not imply either that any wars are right either. It does not even imply that conceivable wars began by a world police force would be right. It leaves open the possibility, indeed the probability, that some past or present wars were or are wholly wrong, and that they outstripped or are outstripping terrorism by far in their savage effects.

If the given conception excludes from political violence the legal activity by policemen and military forces within a society, it certainly *does* include as violence, as already anticipated, the use of force by policemen or military forces or other officers within a society when this is against the law. It evidently also includes, importantly, what has been called *state-violence*. It covers the wounding and killing of unresisting Palestinians in refugee camps by Israeli soldiers in tanks, against international law, quite as readily as it covers the killing of Israelis by suicide bombers. How could any unhypocritically consistent conception or definition fail to cover both things?

There is something else important that violence as conceived can be taken to include. This is so since to *use* force is not necessarily to engage in it yourself. The given conception of violence can be taken to cover what can also be called the instigation of violence. Being the cat of the cat's paw. Political violence therefore includes what has been engaged in by some of our countries, or agencies within them, which is the financing, advising or even creating of armed groups within other societies. Certainly the United States and Britain have engaged in this cat's paw violence. The case of Nicaragua is well-known.

The latter facts are one of several things that lead on to a further and persistent issue we need to consider about the definition of political violence. Our governments and much of our press and other media have been inclined to give a better name to our armed groups in other societies, our cat's paws or proxies. It is not the name of being counter-revolutionaries, as typically they are, but of being freedom-fighters or patriots or something of the sort. Once, many of them could be designated anti-communists. In any case, the idea has been to subtract them from the inevitably suspect category of the politically violent.

What this came to, and still comes to, is an inclination to think and speak of political violence more narrowly than we just have. In effect it is made into *wrongful* political violence. This violence is not only a use of physical force that injures, damages, violates or destroys people or things, but, more than that, it *is* a wrongful use of such force, to be morally condemned and rightly so. It is not merely force for the worse in the first instance, because it damages or destroys, but force that is wrong taking its further upshots and everything else into account. Its often being directed against innocent people is part of this condemnation.

This tendency was strengthened after September 11. The feelings of revulsion for the killers, and also a kind of instinctive strategy, issued in a sometimes tacit but very common conception of all political violence, or the kind of it to which we are coming, *terrorism*, as evil, demented, against civilization, unspeakable, perhaps such as to make possible the torture of those who engage in it. Something like the same impulse has moved those who are against us, some Islamic apologists. They have entered into a conception, concentrated on a kind of violence, of which *they* disapprove or against which *they* have stronger feelings. That kind of violence is the state-violence of Israel against the Palestinians, say in the refugee camps. This is also made at least wrong by definition.

Against all this, calm and orderly political philosophers with the aim of clear-headed thinking and talking have regularly proposed that we do not attempt to restrict political violence to the kind we disapprove of or hate. Their reason is that we and others do not agree in our disapproval and hatred and so we shall be at cross purposes.

Well, I doubt that limiting political violence to a kind we disapprove of would necessarily make thinking much less clear, or much impede discussion, anyway among readers of books. No doubt, too, on a good day, President Bush could keep things straight. He could separate his own idea of political violence from somebody else's. As Mr Blair could, incidentally, after his useful tutorial from President Assad of Syria, on the subject of state-terrorism as against the terrorism preoccupying Mr Blair.

Still, it *is* a good idea to side with the calm and orderly political philosophers. We should not define political violence so as to suit either Mr Bush and Mr Blair or their disapproving tutors. But that is not the end of the matter. It seems to me you can think about writing some *non-partisan* morality into a definition of political violence. You can think about writing a clause about the possible wrongfulness of political violence into the very definition of it.

This would indeed move a little towards begging the question of the moral justification of political violence all things considered, and towards making morally-justified violence a contradiction in terms. But if the inquiry should turn out to have a disconcerting upshot, including the rightfulness of some political violence, then it would not necessarily be the case that we would have a contradiction in terms. What is *possibly* wrong can turn out right.

It seems to me that reminders are good ideas. You have noted that already, in connection with the reality of bad lives. Political violence, simply as violence, and like any violence, is something that injures, damages, violates or destroys people and things, sometimes homes, whole neighbourhoods, public offices, places of worship, or great symbols. It is possible, of course, to distinguish this fact of injury or the like from what we want to keep out of political violence as defined, which is its wrongfulness taking everything into account – necessarily from a certain point of view. Might it be a good idea, then, to write into a definition of violence the explicit reminder that there is a *prima facie* assumption to be made about all violence, which is that it may well be wrong? Such a *prima facie* assumption does follow, doesn't it, from the injury, damage, violation or destruction of people and what they value?

For what it is worth, the political violence I myself would be inclined to have in mind, if we stopped at this point, before getting to terrorism, would be

violence with a political and social intention, raising a question of its moral justification – either illegal violence within a society or smaller-scale violence than war between states or societies and not according to international law.

Terrorism defined

Now terrorism. Does it amount to political violence as now defined along with the additional proviso that it is intended to work at least partly by causing terror – putting many people, maybe much or all of a population, in some kind of fear? So we could decide. This would be terrorism strictly or carefully understood. Before taking any decision, however, we can usefully look at a question or two.

Is there any political violence as so far understood that is *not* intended to work by causing terror or fear? Yes, there has been violence very different from the attacks of September 11, which presumably *were* aimed partly at causing personal fear among many Americans and related feelings among all Americans. Very different from this violence has been violence directed specifically at a head of state, or politicians, soldiers or policemen. The latter violence certainly causes a different and lesser apprehension among people generally.

Also, in Northern Ireland, decades of bombings and shootings eventually gave rise to a kind of resigned or quiet fear, something like an accepted condition of life. It is closer to the mark to say that this political violence, in addition to being a matter of hatred and vengeance, eventually aimed to secure social ends not by putting people generally in lively fear, but simply by killing people. That is, the situation was more akin to armed struggle or war than the American situation after September 11.

It is clear enough, then, that there is political violence about which it would be misleading to say that it intends to achieve its end by way of causing general fear. We do presumably want to include this sort of violence in our thinking. The Irish killings are part of our subject-matter, as are such killings elsewhere. So too do we want to include any future violence against America with the same roots and ends as September 11, but not such violence as to cause fear among Americans generally for their own safety. Killing the President or American embassy people in Africa must come to mind.

Political violence so far conceived, pretty ordinarily conceived, is certain violence within a society or between societies, taken as justified by political and social ends, about which a moral question immediately arises. This clearly includes political violence not aimed at terror. That is one fact. What is also true, despite calm and orderly philosophers, is that the term 'terrorism' has been put to use to cover all of what we have so far conceived as political violence. 'Terrorism' is used for more than terrorism strictly or carefully understood. That is now ordinary usage or an implication of ordinary usage. One reason for this general use of the term 'terrorism', plainly, is that it has more condemnation in it than 'political violence'. It conveys an additional and calculating motive to the perpetrators.

What we need here in our inquiry, to bring this necessary fussing about terms to an end, is some muscular decision-making. We can give up on the strict and careful idea of terrorism, and go on as in fact we began in our inquiry, with a more general idea of it. We can speak of one thing as either *terrorism* or *political violence*, making no difference between the two terms.

That thing is

violence with a political and social intention, whether or not intended to put people in general in fear, and raising a question of its moral justification – either illegal violence within a society or smaller-scale violence than war between states or societies and not according to international law.

That is our final definition.

Do you want excuses for giving the name of terrorism to the sort of violence that isn't intended to put people in general into fear? You can say that making people in general fearful isn't the *main* thing about the other sort. The main thing is getting political and social change, something about the great goods. So the two sorts are more alike than may be thought. You can say too that both the first sort, and incidentally war, certainly do have *an* aim having to do with fear. But the main excuse is the recommendation of going along with a common usage.

As in the case of the earlier definition of political violence, things have to be kept in mind.

Like all other definitions for use in thinking, rather than for use in international or other politics, our definition of terrorism does not by itself morally condemn in a final way everything that falls under it. It leaves open the possibility that there was justification of, say, the particular terrorism that led to the existence of the state of Israel. So with the attempt on Hitler's life' and attempts to kill Osama bin Laden in the years before September 11. It is like a definition of killing that does not by itself make all killing wrong, including execution by the state and killing in real self-defence.

The terrorism defined does of course include state-terrorism. The definition leaves open whether state-terrorism has been the larger and more destructive part of terrorism as defined and whether our wars have been worse than terrorism, which of course they have. The terrorism defined also includes cat's paw terrorism, i.e. terrorism by the cat as distinct from the paw.

Something else was not remarked on before, with political violence. The definition of terrorism does not get in the way of our looking for something at least as useful to us. It does not get in the way of our looking for suitable language for states and societies that by omission shorten or drag down multitudes of lives. We are not well-served by our language here, whatever the explanation of the fact.

There is a greater need for suitable language since our final definition of terrorism is not so general as to include what fell under violence and terrorism as often defined in the past by our critics. Our definition does not include bad or worse treatment of social or economic classes not including the use of force. This was *structural violence* or *institutional violence*. That would include not only racism and various special kinds of victimization but also the arrangement or at any rate the situation summed up in such facts as one noticed earlier, that the best-off tenth of Americans has 30.5 per cent of America's total income or consumption and the worst-off tenth has 1.8 per cent. Structural violence is an arrangement that issues in bad lives.

It is certainly possible to understand someone's determination that his moral view of situations and arrangements should not be impeded by language itself, by the mere fact that terms of opprobrium have by custom come to be useable only by his opponents, or best used by them. But there is a clear difference between the use of force and other practices, however vicious and destructive the latter may be. It is worth marking the distinction, as well as resolving to make good use of other resources of language. What is non-violent can be more destructive than violence. Think of disease for a start, or the viciousness of loans that leave a family destitute, or loans that do that to a good part of a whole country. Our definition of terrorism does not rule out the possibility that some terrorism could be justified as a response to what others called structural violence.

We will come back to that sort of thing, but our subject now is the wrongfulness of the terrorism at the Twin Towers again.

Why some say September 11 was wrong

Whatever is to be said of wrong or right with terrorism in general, or such examples as the terrorism that led to the founding of the state of Israel, and the new South Africa after apartheid, and a society fairer to Catholics in Northern Ireland, and, to look further back, the United States of America itself, we have it settled that the terrorism of September 11 *was* wrong. We look for stronger words about it, and can find them.

This leaves a question open. It is the question of *why* the terrorism of September 11 was wrong. It has more in it than any proposition to the effect that two wrongs, the first being our own with respect to the bad lives, do not make a right. It is a subject more important than you may first suppose.

It is such partly because it will be a prelude to other things that will come after it, the end of this inquiry. To get a mistaken answer to the question of why September 11 was wrong would likely be to store up additional failure. To get a correct answer will help us to deal with the last questions. One will be that of how the subject of moral responsibility for the day of September 11 comes together with the wrong we ourselves have done with multitudes of lives cut short, weak, degraded, respectless or thin. There will also be the question of what we did after September 11, and of what to do now.

Why were the killings of September 11 wrong? That is, what is the reason or explanation or ground for the invincible feelings that they were wrong? One of these feelings, as you have heard, was a horror owed to entering into the fear of the victims, people in an extreme situation. Other feelings, lately recalled, had to do with the violation of the agreement between us all that is the fact and practice of natural morality, and with the self-indulgence or worse of inconsistency, and with the real truths about human existence at the bottom of morality. Those truths have to do with suffering and the like.

So – we have necessary feelings about September 11. We can ask about the content of these feelings about killings, the reasons or propositions in them, their particular sources in facts. As you have heard, it is essential to know. Not to know, even if a judgement is right, is then to be wandering or even blundering around, unable to see what goes with that right judgement or does not go with it – what other feelings we ought to have or ought not to have about other things, maybe ourselves. Help is certainly on offer. To the question of the content or whatever of our feelings about September 11, we are not short of answers and of talk that implies answers. Most are general convictions about terrorism applied to September 11.

The first answer is simply that terrorism is *violence*. Being such it is not one of a number of things that are rational, reasonable, a matter of reason rather than power or force. These better ways of going on and conducting yourself include negotiation, discussion, argument, compromise, arbitration, respect for the views of others, attempting to understand those views, willingness to be shown wrong, and so on. The philosopher of science Karl Popper of the London School of Economics, an advocate of what he called the open society, gave the first answer firmly in an essay called 'Utopia and Violence' and could find no refutation of it. Reason, he said, is the precise opposite of violence and power.

This line of thought, which typically does not distinguish clearly between violence and other uses of force, does not take us far. We can all agree that it is very often better to come to an agreement than to fight. Yet we often fight, and believe it to be rational and right. The history of nations is a history of fighting, and certainly we are still at it. Are there many Americans convinced that their government should have carried on negotiating, or at any rate gone on threatening longer, after September 11?

What then is this rationality or whatever that is always served by negotiation or whatever? We must hope, on behalf of Professor Popper, that the rationality or whatever is not identical with the negotiation or whatever. There is reason to suspect that he has fallen into such a circular argument. Other seemingly high-minded opponents of violence do not do better in supplying us with the sense in which violence, and it half-seems other uses of force, are all to be understood as irrational. It would be hard for them to do so. It would be hard for them to explain how it is that negotiation or whatever always does have some high recommendation of rationality.

Certainly it would be hard to explain to a young student in Zambia that the half-lives and quarter-lives around him have the recommendation of rationality since they are, to a considerable extent, the fruit of international negotiation. So too with a young student in Palestine, who has already had some experience of international negotiation. Or a student in Sauda Arabia who takes it that his culture and in particular his religion, not to mention his people, are brought into disrespect by a profitable alliance between us and his royal family. He will not be overwhelmed by the proposition that the alliance is the fruit of negotiation. The three students, rather, will be suspicious of the highmindedness.

So am I. Another reason is that it forgets about our own violence. It forgets about all of the past in that respect. It forgets about what goes on as these pages are written, a good while after the war of 1991 with Iraq was finished. What goes on is the continued bombing of that country. This seems to be, among other things, our British government's forgetfulness that our League of Nations mandate of 1920 to run the place also ended some time ago.

A momentarily better answer to the question of why the September 11 acts of terrorism were wrong is the simple one that they were *killings*. That is a moral simplicity, it may be said, but it is also inescapable. In fact, if it has some reality about it, it is too simple. The ground of our feelings cannot be just the fact of killing, since there are killings we tolerate and do not condemn. There have been wars that were right. Some of us, Americans above all, take lives of others in the ordinary operation of the machinery of punishment by the state.

Are such killings as those of September 11 wrong because they were of innocents, or, if you are tough-minded, of non-combatants? There is a difference. Such thoughts have immediate and greater force. But, as inevitably, they face the reply that some killings of innocents or non-combatants, if not much defended, are not condemned. Innocents are killed in just wars. Innocents have been killed by us in Afghanistan. What is said in excuse is of course that their deaths were not the first intention of their killers, but necessary in the carrying out of another intention, a justified one.

Exactly that, however, is the argument on behalf of such killers as those of September 11. That the argument can be defeated is my conviction. That it can be defeated merely by relying on the innocence of people killed is sadly not the case. Consistency stands in the way, and it cannot be passed by or disdained. Does anyone need reminding that consistency is not a small and overridable matter of tidy-mindedness or the like? It is another necessity. To speak both for and against something, as one does in inconsistency, is to say one thing that must be false. To think both for and against something, as one does in inconsistency, is to think nothing. To go on speaking both for and against something is to say nothing.

One other answer to the question of why such terrorist killings are wrong is that they are *killings by individuals*, as distinct from killings by states or nations, for which there is something to be said. There seems little doubt that our ordinary reactions to such terrorism as that of September 11 owe much to this fact. This distinction between killings by individuals and killings by authorities requires ignorance and forgetfulness. There *is* state-terrorism, of greater and more terrible effect than other terrorism. There is also unspeakable killing by the states that is not terrorism as defined. There were unspeakable killings, some millions of them, killings on a new scale, by the German state. To look further into history, any century of it, is to find more evidence that destroys any attempt to think of killing by a state as generally justified or legitimated.

The point intended, however, may not be to the effect that the state is in general justified in killing. It may be that only a state's killings have a possibility of justification. That it is a state rather than a self-appointed individual taking a life is a required or necessary condition, not a sufficient one, of the killing being justified.

Clearly this is no better. We know of too much killing that is not by the state, and thus does not satisfy the necessary condition, but is not condemned by us. For a start, we instigate or accept or tolerate uprisings against what we regard as awful or dangerous states. It would have been all right for the plotters to kill Hitler. Throughout history such uprisings against one kind of government or another have had moral support into which almost all of us now enter. Is there any modern state that was not born in blood? Is there any decent state that was not?

It thus seems that a condemnation of terrorism cannot rest on a number of things. It cannot rest on its being irrational in not being negotiation and the like, or its being illegal, or its being killing, or killing of innocents, or not sanctioned by some nation state. These and other reasons offered against terrorism, however, may be thought to recover strength when brought together with another and larger ground of condemnation.

It may be thought, for example, that there is more to be said against terrorism that goes against negotiation with *a certain kind* of nation state. It may be thought that there is particular wrong in killing citizens or innocent citizens of a certain kind of state and society. It may be thought, above all, that terrorism is to be condemned when it attacks such a state and society. That is a *democratic* state and society. Our democracies are special. In themselves and of their nature they are involved in negotiation and compromise. Their laws are to be respected. They are not like other states. They constitute or are most or much of *civilization*.

Democracy

There seems little doubt that we were affected by the attack on the Twin Towers partly because, whatever its rationale in the minds of the attackers, it was an attack on a democracy. Certainly this fact was much heard of from our democratic leaders. In so doing they were not only being politicians speaking for their own line of life, but engaging in a general kind of thinking that can be reasonable enough. When there are two parties engaged in a dispute about right and wrong, and there are arguments to and fro, it is pretty reasonable to suppose there is something more in the arguments of the party that has some intrinsic and general recommendation. In court, we put more trust in a witness of good character than one of bad character.

If kinds of states and societies can be rated, as they can from the point of view of any social morality, and it emerges that one kind is superior, more in accord in its nature with a principle or principles that ought to govern life, then its reasons have a kind of recommendation, deserve an attention. Further, and more simply, the very nature of such a government and society is a special reason for an attack on it being wrong. We engaged in a world war to save democracy, and almost all of us have at least regretted the extinguishing of democracies by others or ourselves.

Thus there is the general possibility of a reasoned condemnation of some terrorism and of September 11 in particular. It depends, of course, on what can actually be said for democracy. The novelist E.M. Forster is remembered for giving only two cheers for it. Maybe he had in mind that it attracts politicians educated only in the law, even party leaders. But this light-heartedness has to give way, in a serious inquiry, to a real question. As these lines are being written, my *International Herald Tribune* carries news, yet again, of scandal in and about democracy. This time it has to do with more details of the Enron corporation's influence on American democracy, to say nothing of English democracy and also Prince Charles. International adversaries of ours, not all of them mad, have over decades condemned our democracy as a sham.

Is it possible to detach a little from this sort of thing and to come to a reasoned summary of our systems of democracy in the United States, Britain and so on? Are there general facts that support such a summary? Can they do the job without raising up either a suspicion of piety and patriotism or a suspicion of conspiracy theory?

You were detained earlier, reader, and perhaps were patient, in connection with the definition of terrorism. Now we need to take longer over democracy than you may think is necessary. The reason is that our democracies have much to do with our current question and also with more. Our democracies and their nature and particular facts within them will bear heavily on our remaining still larger questions, about our responsibility and what to do – what to do where that is not just what to do about terrorism. As well, to come to a true view of our democracies will be to throw a light on the past of this inquiry in which we find ourselves. It will give us a further understanding of our omissions with respect to the short lives and the other lacks or denials of great goods.

I cannot confidently anticipate your agreement with me on a summary of our democracy. But you may well agree we need something plainer than Abraham Lincoln's fine hope for a government conceived in liberty and dedicated to equality, a government of, by, and for the people. As an emigrant American, Joseph Schumpeter, pointed out later, to say that it is a government *by* the people, that the *people* govern, is to go too far, indeed into plain falsehood. It is the government that does the governing, whatever the people do.

You can make a better if less edifying start by taking up a more realistic idea of democracy. You can say that democracy is the procedure or practice of which three things are true. The first has to do with freedom or liberty, the second with equality, and the third with those two things being in a way effective.

1. The people hear proposals from individuals among them who are free to come forward as candidates for government. They can offer any views or politics. The people freely choose among them in an election. Then the people influence the elected government as they want, maybe making them feel unpopular enough to give up.

2. The individuals just mentioned have an equal right to stand as candidates and to get an equal hearing from the people for whatever proposals. There is the absolute equality in the election of *one person, one vote*. There is an equal right afterwards to get at the government and change its mind.

3. The government does indeed govern. That is not only to say that it takes the decisions, by majority vote again. What happens in the society, so far as it is up to anybody, is decided by the government rather than anyone or anything behind the scenes. What happens has the recommendation of being owed to freedom and equality.

The trouble with this more realistic idea of democracy is that if you really think of Washington or London, let alone Texas or London's rotten borough of Westminster as it was, doubts creep in, at every point. They creep in about each of freedom, equality, and governmental power.

Is it only their funny proposals that keep some individuals among us from being real candidates? Does it instead have something to do with a consensus of assumption and feeling that is not entirely a matter of open-minded reflection but has to do with the ownership of television stations and networks? In which case, does the idea of the freedom in democracy with respect to candidates and proposals to the people need qualification?

With respect to the people, there is also the matter that the free choosing of a government is not done by them. It is not done by *the people* as that term might carelessly be understood. The voting is done by much less than all the people, maybe about half. This half includes a lot more people with such advantages, however well earned, as cars to get them to the voting booth, and maybe education. When elections are close, as often they are, this is particularly important. It is certainly not as if we can have the reassurance that the upshot would be the same if everybody freely made it to the booth.

Perhaps more fundamentally, although it is impossible to separate the matters of freedom and equality, doubts creep in about the equality. Does the electorate have an equal chance of hearing each of the views they would pay attention to under better conditions? *One person, one vote* is fine, and it is right that we go on celebrating it. But what is the rule for influence on the government after the election? It's true that we all have an equal legal right, which is to say that there isn't a law against some of us having a go, but is a citizen or a whole neighbourhood on the same ground as a newspaper columnist or a corporation with its lobbyists?

In thinking about this, you can't really detach from the general facts of which the Enron corporation was a salient example. In Britain you may think back to the chap in the dark glasses who runs European car racing. He gave my old party, now Mr Blair's New Labour Party, a million quid, for which Mr Blair was grateful. Not so grateful as then to do Mr Ecclestone a good turn about tobacco advertising, which thing did in fact happen but would have happened anyway. We have Mr Blair's word for that.

And if anybody or anything behind the scenes does have something to do with what actually happens in a democratic society, is it all equal? Is it all equal between Mr Rupert Murdoch of the newspapers and yourself, or between the Ford Motor Company or the American Legion and an equal number of whoever else, maybe university teachers or unmarried mothers, or people in Idaho without private health insurance?

So we all know, when we're actually trying to think, and not doing politics overtly or covertly, that the more realistic idea of democracy we've been contemplating in place of Lincoln's hope is not very realistic. We need to do better.

One step has been taken by the industry of political scientists who work on democracy. They have focused on something else it is possible to forget, that in our societies individuals come together into groups, or at any rate can be thought of in groups. They come together into or at any rate are in one or another group with a common interest. If you want to explain more or less anything about a society, you need to attend to them. You get somewhere in thinking about gun laws by thinking of the part of the population that has a gun.

So the point is that if you want to characterize democracy, and even more if you want to try to explain what comes out of it, turn your attention to interest-groups. Some will be organized and some not. They will be of different kinds. Some will be workers in a certain industry, some will live in a region or other piece of geography, some will be highminded and some low. Some will have allegiances to wider ethnic groups or races, or their ethnic group in another country. Some will be property-owners, some will be liberals, some will be members of unions, and so on down to our estimable vegetarians.

There are some other steps towards a conception of democracy more realistic than the one looked at, but the most necessary one has indeed to do with equality. If you take into account that you can't read the papers or watch the news without knowing that democracy isn't as equal as all that, you can come to the standard enlightened idea of democracy, most common among the readers of books. It has many variations but comes to something like this.

1. Candidates supported and influenced by interest-groups propose themselves freely for government and are freely chosen by interest-groups. Those elected are thereafter also freely influenced in this way. That is not to say that what happens is not because of individuals, but rather to describe and take account of individuals in the most explanatory way.

2. There is *approximate equality*, something like equality, in the competition involving interest-groups to become a real candidate. There is the absolute equality of one person one vote in the election. There is *approximate equality* in the influencing of the resulting government by the interest-groups.

3. Decisions of government come out of the machinery just sketched. These decisions, as against those of large corporations, are reasonably effective with respect to what happens in the society. If not everything is above board, it isn't mainly under the board.

It is not only such news as that of Mr Ecclestone's piece of good luck that leads to the standard enlightened conception of democracy. It is also the settled thought, in the opposite direction, that what makes democracy different from all other systems of government is the equality and freedom of it. That is the difference between us and the remaining communists, for a start. If reading the papers leads to watering down the equality content, the settled thought keeps equality there and works to make more of it.

As already implied, by the way, there is a close connection between the equality and the freedom. My political and other freedom and yours are related. Mine is fixed by how much you have. If we have the same amount, putting aside any other complications, we are each free. If you have half of the freedom I have, are you really free? I am going to get my way a lot of the time. Are you free at all if we are *more* unequal in freedom – if, say, it can be quantified, and I have eight times as much? It isn't as if equality is in general inconsistent or in conflict with freedom. In general they go together. The same is to be said of the dim old idea that there is a general conflict between equality and individual liberties.

Hierarchic democracy

We need to get down to something else, which is more thinking about the interest-groups. We need to think some more about the approximate equality in political power. The vegetarians, maybe sadly, have never decided an election. Who has? What groups? Almost all of them in the course of time? That is the question. There are a lot of books answering it. Shouldn't all the answers come down to the proposition that what groups decide things has a lot to do with money? Don't all opinions really agree on that? Even if not all opinions are well-informed about the details?

Never having been a Marxist or a half-Marxist or a student of

Marx or a market-Marxist, I myself have no left-over affection for Karl's theory of history, which is economic determinism. The theory somehow explains everything, including who wins democratic elections. It does the explaining by way of something called productive relations in a society (e.g. capitalism), these being the result of the productive forces underneath (e.g. the steam engine or the computer). Nor do I think everybody has only material motives.

But, having my head screwed on frontwards, I share with you the awareness that money does more than talk. Interest-groups defined in terms of money must be very important in understanding our democracy. They must be important in explaining the policies, practices and other facts to which it gives rise.

Return to the table of figures back at the beginning (p. 8). Some of the inequalities in it, those in the last two columns, are between groups of people in our democratic societies. The worst-off tenth of Americans, the tenth that has the least of America's total income and consumption, has the insignificant *1.8 per cent* of that total. The tenth that has the most has no less than *30.5 per cent* of the total.

So there is an inequality that comes to one group having about seventeen times as much as another of what is going in the country. Another way of looking at it, involving a different definition and more recent figures, gives the top tenth of Americans *41.2 per cent* and the bottom *four tenths* 10.5 per cent. The bottom tenth in the way we are looking at things, for various reasons, will have less than 1.8 per cent.*

For Britain, the past inequality in incomes has been such that the top tenth has about ten or eleven times as much as the bottom. It will not have decreased. My party has carried on in government where the Conservatives left off. There are new initiatives announced weekly that will transform something, maybe the railways or the schools or the dire condition of the underfunded National Health Service, but the poor are still getting poorer and the rich richer. Yes, that's right. The poor are still getting poorer and the rich richer. In this spring of 2002, that is the known sum of my party in power, my party that

* Edward N. Wolff (2000), 'Recent Trends in Wealth Ownership, 1983–1998', Working Paper no. 300, Table 2, Jerome Levy Economics Institute.

established the National Health Service and did so much about poverty. For an indication of the state of things in other countries, look back to the table.

There should be something else in the table, about all our well-off countries. But books and life aren't perfect, and economists aren't perfect in getting together to produce comparable figures. And there is a tendency to think about our incomes rather than something else. In fact the table has a hole in it.

To start at home, I not only have a monthly income but I have some money in the Nationwide Building Society. There is enough there to be called *wealth*, which subject is not in the table. I get some interest or income from it, but I recently also spent some of it on my family and on another more public cause. I spent a good chunk of this capital, as people can and do. A bigger chunk is staying there for a rainy day, but I could spend a lot more and probably will, as people can and do. One way of escaping death taxes, as Mr Fisher my financial advisor ruminatively says. So wealth can and does turn into money to spend, on what you want.

Wealth in houses and the like, not money, is also of benefit in various ways. If I am not mistaken I get a little more attention from the officer of local government looking at our application to replace a stone balustrade because I'm well-heeled. After all, if he turns down the application carelessly or unfairly, then even if my income dries up for a while, I can still call on the Nationwide and hire a lawyer or an architect to get after him.

This vignette is as good a way as any of showing that the table should have in it something about shares of wealth held by different sections of population in a society. That would have been relevant at several moments of our inquiry before now, but forget that. Let me rectify things a bit in connection with our present subject, which is interest-groups in a democracy and, as you will expect, their different powers.

America as a society stands out from the rest or most of us in connection with the distribution of wealth – although we in Britain are catching up, if that is the right verb. America's total marketable wealth is assets minus debts, or rather assets that are readily exchangeable for money minus the debts. Who has how much of it? Who has what percentages of the total?

In the most recent year for which figures are to hand, the *top one tenth* of Americans had *71 per cent* of it. The bottom *four tenths* taken together had a lot less than 1 per cent. They had *0.2 per cent.**

This gives you the result that the top tenth had *a few thousand times* as much wealth as the bottom four tenths. What about the bottom tenth? They exist, and they want and need things. They want and need the great goods as much as we all do. And, whether or not they think of it, they miss the one we're now concerned with, having to do with freedom and power. It would make a difference to them. So how little does the bottom tenth in America have of the wealth of America?

Well, do a little calculating for yourself, and come up with how many times more wealth the top tenth has than the bottom if the top tenth, as we know, has about 71 per cent. Start from the additional fact that in wealth the bottom tenth has *nothing or less than nothing* – zero or negative net worth. You know in advance you are not going to conclude that the top tenth has only *a few thousand times* as much wealth as the bottom tenth. The inequality won't be as small as that.

A conclusion to be drawn about the American and other democracies and the standard enlightened idea of them is pretty plain. It rests on the thought we may share, even if another book could be written about it, that the interest-groups to concentrate on in characterizing our democracies are interest-groups defined in terms of income and wealth. And, further, you can actually identify these groups as the tenths of population sharing the total income and wealth. They are real groups of real people, with addresses.

There are also other definable interest-groups, obviously, but those in terms of income and wealth matter immensely more. Further, if you think of other interest-groups that count a lot, because of their history or their degree of organization or whatever, they overlap a lot with the interest-groups in terms of wealth and income.

* Edward N. Wolff (2000), 'Recent Trends in Wealth Ownership, 1983–1998', Working Paper no. 300, Table 2, Jerome Levy Economics Institute.

The interest-groups in terms of wealth and income are not equal, or more or less equal. They are not approximately equal, as I used to say myself. They are not half-equal, or anything like equal. That is an abuse of language that is a falsehood. What they are, if you stick to the English language as we have it, is *absolutely unequal*. As a result, to come to the conclusion, democracies are not only misunderstood in Lincoln's good hope, and in what seemed a more realistic idea of them, but also in the standard enlightened idea of them.

A hierarchy, for present purposes, is an organization or system in which people or groups of people are ranked not only in terms of status or authority but also power. Those on the top get their way over those below. Our democracies, given the facts we now have before us, about a ranking of tenths of population from top to bottom, are rightly understood as hierarchies. The form of government we have is *hierarchic democracy*. The kind of society we have is *hierarchic democracy*. What we have in our democracies is roughly as follows.

1. Interest-groups in terms of higher income and wealth are dominant in limiting the range of real candidates and choices in an election, and dominant in influencing who gets elected. These interest-groups are also dominant in the influencing of the government after the election.

2. In this influencing, there is gross inequality, nothing like equality, between all the interest-groups. It is reasonable to take a top interest-group of ten to have at least hundreds of times the influence of the bottom group.

3. What happens in the society is owed in part to decisions of the government and in part to corporations, business and money. Insofar as what happens is not owed to government, it is again owed to a dominance of groups of higher income and wealth.

The reflective reader will notice that this, the hierarchic conception of our democracies, needs filling in. What exactly does 'dominant' mean in the first sentence and thereafter? Fortunately, however, it is already an English word with a pretty good meaning. What more can be said in support of the central proposition about at least hundreds of times more influence at the top? Quite a lot. I still hope to fulfill that promise to have a look at the business or financial side of our societies. Also, what precisely is the idea of political power allied to the idea of financial or economic power? With most of these and some other questions, the reflective reader will have to wait for another day, or do some work himself, or herself. The work may not result in precision that will satisfy all parties.

But it will not defeat the hierarchic conception, only give it detail.

Why September 11 was wrong

Hierarchic democracy is better than some things, better than many past things. It is better than what we instigated or helped bring about in Chile in 1973, which was the murdering and torturing government of General Pinochet. Maybe hierarchic democracy does not deserve another name that comes to mind, that of *oligarchic democracy*. It is akin to a state being governed by a small group, akin to Aristotle's rule by a few in their own interest. There is room for more reflection on that subject, and on the subject of how understandable it is that such governments should be principal agents of our omissions with respect to the bad lives. There is room for more reflection on the economic side of our democracy, business and capitalism, but not now. We need now to come to another conclusion, on what has been our main question for a while.

The conclusion is that there is no simple objection of a certain kind to terrorism against us, even the terrorism of September 11. We do not have a certain imagined moral high ground to stand on in condemning terrorism against us, in explaining our revulsion for the killers at the Twin Towers. Our democracies do not give us that. They do not come very near to giving us that. What condemns the killers of 3,000 people on September 11 was *not* that they offended against democracy.

That is cant, and will remain so no matter how often it is uttered by our politicians. What condemns the killers could not be that they offended against those degrees of equality and freedom that are the reality of our democracies. That would be to say that what condemns them is that they offended against practices and rules, indeed a way

115

of living, that enshrines nothing other than gross inequalities and therefore denials of freedom.

The general conclusion about our democracies has been drawn from indubitable inequalities in income and wealth and hence in political power. It is hard to resist a reminder of something else, about what our democracies do or produce. You find out about the nature of a system from its record of behaviour, so to speak. Some say that is the very best way, as in the case of the nature of a person. You also find out about a system's recommendation.

One thing we know about our democracies is that they have for decades kept our own distributions of wealth and income within our societies pretty much as they are, despite a recent trend to greater inequality. Another thing is that they are now principal arrangers of the bad lives, the world as it is, that sample loss of 20 million years of living time. Our democracies are deadly states.

Do you want to say that there is the qualification or consolation that each of our democracies does better by its own people? Does better by its own people than other forms of government do by theirs? That this tells a different truth about our lives? You might then pay another visit to the table of figures (p. 8), and look again at the inequalities in income, and keep in mind what has just been noticed about wealth. You can also find out other things of relevance.

As of the other year the average length of life for an American white was 77.3 years. The average length of life for an American black or African American was 71.3 years.* Six years' difference on average then, an average brought down by very many lives shorter than 71.3 years. But just think about the average. I was 69 yesterday, and have a hope about going on for a while. I suppose blacks do too. Six years would make a difference. The loss of six years on average makes a difference. There are about 30 million American blacks.

Are you English or Welsh? Do you think we do things better? Not according to the national statistics. We are divided into five of what are called social classes, in fact occupational classes, from professional

---

* *National Vital Statistics Report* (2001), vol. 48, no. 18, 7 Feb., p. 33, National Center for Health Statistics.

down through managerial and so on to unskilled. The latest figures show that professional men have average lifetimes of 78.5 years. Unskilled men have average lifetimes of 71.1 years.* That is well over seven years' difference. You will know that although it is relatively small, there are a lot of men in the unskilled class. About 1,500,000 in fact.

So – it isn't the case that the wrong of September 11 was that it was an offence against democracy. Did many of us think the attack was wrong because it was an offence against the economic as against the political side of our existence? An offence against what traditionally has been called capitalism? No doubt some of us have had this feeling, maybe a determined reaction to the fact that the attack was against the two buildings that were the outstanding symbols of capitalism or big business, the World Trade Centre. We will in a way come back to the subject, but not spend time now on the idea that the attack was wrong for the supposed reasons, wrong on account of the same fact seemingly used by others in trying to justify it.

Given the view just come to of our democracies, and things said earlier about morality and moralities, it will not take long to deliver some other conclusions about the wrong of September 11.

One true reason why the killers of September 11 rightly have our revulsion is that they violated the natural fact and practice of morality. That is a fact and practice that is far from perfectly consistent, so it is not something such that any of us can approve of all of it, but that is not the only truth about it. It is a kind of foundation of life, though, a source of decency, a source of civilization. Some of it, having to do with killing, has to pass into any system of morality worked out from it.

For me, and perhaps you, the killers of September 11 are condemned more clearly and explicitly by one thing worked out from the natural practice, which is to say the morality of humanity. The killers are not best condemned as a kind of deduction from uncertain principles, principles at a certain height above life, as in the

---

* 'Trends in Life Expectancy by Social Class, 1972–1999' (2002), Table 1, Office for National Statistics.

case of liberalism and other social moralities. The killers are not condemned by any morality of special obligation, for reasons you know. They are condemned by the principle of humanity, that we are to save people from bad lives. They are condemned by a principal policy of this humanity, a prohibition on wounding, attack, killing and other violence and near-violence. This condemnation is not qualified by the policy's not being simple, as the condemnation of killing in natural morality is not qualified by that condemnation not being simple.

It is no more an unthinkingly absolute policy than any other sustainable one. It is human and so does not fail to see that if it ever were actually the case that there was a choice that had to be made between many killings and few, the few could not possibly be avoided in the interest of clean hands. It is not out of touch with the reality we find ourselves in. It is not unthinking, either, in supposing that it is possible to do the right thing without struggling to come to the best judgement as to the probable effects of an action or line of action. There can be no sustainable principle that lifts us out of the world, out of the need to try to see what will or would happen in it. Any morality that made things simple would be wrong. We know things are not simple.

It is to be allowed, too, that the policy against killing and other violence has to be articulated so as not to prohibit self-defence and no doubt more than that. Even an ideal society would need to protect itself. Consistent with that is the fact the codification will not conceivably make another exception for massacre. This policy, to make use again of the idea of ostensive definition, will not be framed independently of such a massacre as that of September 11. Rather, it will in part be derived from it.

Despite not being simple, the morality of humanity leaves no question about the wrong done on September 11. What was done was wrong because there could be no certainty or significant probability, no reasonable hope, that it would work to secure a justifying end, but only a certainty that it would destroy lives. Reason, which is to say reflective intelligence, as distinct from moral bitterness and rage, could not possibly give the conclusion that the attack would have sufficient good consequences, be a real step in that direction. Reflective intelligence had to give the conclusion that it would destroy lives. To carry out the attack, at best, was to do what was horrible. It was, at best, to *gamble* with the lives of very many people – not to risk them, of course, but to take and extinguish them, to use them in gambling.

The killers and those behind them, more particularly, could not know that the killing of several thousand people would in due course serve the end of the principle of humanity, saving people from bad lives. They could have no such rational confidence. Rather, some probability attached to the killing in due course having the opposite effect. The attack could be made use of as a pretext and whatever else, as indeed it was by Israel. It could lead to war. What they did know was that the immediate effect would be awful to the principle of humanity, awful given its equal concern for each of those first victims.

If people are not flies, they are not dice either.

You will think of adding, perhaps, that the killers of September 11, putting aside the ignorance in which they culpably and awfully acted, did not actually have the goal that is the goal of the morality of humanity. They did not strike against the general fact of lives cut short, weak, degraded, respectless or thin. They did not strike against this general fact as much about Africa as anywhere else. If there can be such a thing as terrorism for humanity, this was not it. The aims of the killers, enunciated by bin Laden whatever his role in what they did, had to do with the crime in Palestine, our prolonged attacks on Iraq and its people, and what is perceived as the desecration of a great religion by American oil-dealings with the ruling family of Saudi Arabia. In any case, an intrusion for profit into the homeland of the people of Saudi Arabia and the culture of all Muslims.

Is it possible to think that these aims are close enough to the goal of the morality of humanity? Intentions in our actions can have a particularity about them and also a goal shared with other particular intentions. Is it possible to suppose that the September 11 attacks had nothing at all to do with the omissions of America and of ourselves of which we know, nothing to do with Malawi, Mozambique, Zambia and Sierra Leone? That these were not a necessary context of the particular intentions having to do with Palestine, Iraq and Saudi Arabia? In thinking about it, remember that the attacks on the towers were indeed attacks on the principal symbols of world capitalism.

We need not dispute this question. Whether or not the killers of September 11 are to be thought of as moved by the principle of humanity, they earned their condemnation as hideous and monstrous.

As you will gather, this carries a judgement on conceivable terrorism in no way ambiguous. What I have in mind is such and as many killings as those of September 11, say by the same means and in our world as it is, but indubitably with the goal of the principle of humanity. It is not easy to be brief in this speculation. The conceivable terrorism, to come up for consideration at all, would indeed need to have particularity about it. Let us suppose that particularity would have to do first with Malawi, Mozambique, Zambia and Sierra Leone.

It is plain that such an attack would be at least as wrong as the attack of September 11. If its goal would in a degree be more indisputable, this would not come near to making it right. It would not be right because it would not be rational. It could not be judged of it that it would actually in any degree or way serve the end. On the contrary, it could in the long run impede any progress towards that end. In the short run, it would with certainty destroy lives. Again it would be repulsive and inhuman to act on a hope or chance.

This speculation on some conceivable terrorism is not an idle one. Like the judgement on the actual horror at the Twin Towers, it bears on our last questions. These have to do with our own situation with respect to the actual and the possible massacres, and with what we have done since September 11, and with what is to be done now.

5
Our responsibility,
and what to do

Moral confidence

My moral confidence, my confidence in my moral feelings and judgements, is not so firm now as it was back at the beginning of these reflections. Is your confidence made of sterner stuff? Maybe it shouldn't be. Maybe there are things that should give us both pause. Looking back, there they are, or there they seem to be, marking our route, maybe calling us back.

Take the bad lives of very many people. The lives cut off at ages when you and I had futures, or the lives lacking any material comfort, or lives not free but invaded and oppressed, or without respect and self-respect, or with so little of each of the great goods that they are faint imitations of our lives, ghosts of lives. You too, I trust, were affected by the fact of our wrong in this connection, our having a responsibility for the bad lives.

Some say that we need not be affected, or so affected. The nineteenth-century German philosopher Friedrich Nietzsche stands out among them. He gets more attention than he once did. Certainly he disdained or would disdain the morality of humanity – as coming from, feeding on and issuing in weakness, meekness, resentment or other insufficiently virile conditions. He was of course superior to Christianity, of whose God he famously announced the death. We need not follow his further discourses on the unnaturalness of resisting selfishness, and on slave-moralities as against master-moralities, the need to affirm your own life against others, the inevitability of a will to power, the overman or superman, and so on.

Instead of filling out this vignette, we can instead ask a calmer question about the possibility of a certain condition, *an excess of empathy*. Do I feel too much about the bad lives? Have I invited you to feel too much? Is it also false feeling, hypocrisy? Is it a better idea to do what more sensible and realistic persons do? Feel that while it has to be admitted that a lot of Africans and others haven't got what we have, that's the luck of the draw, the way the world is? Remember that we didn't draw up the original plan, and that everybody makes the best of what they've got? It's all sad, but what is there to do but be sympathetic and not superior, and give what you can spare to Oxfam?

Moral confidence can be touched, too, by more strictly philosophical uncertainties. To have argued for the worked-out morality of humanity as against other such moralities, without giving attention to the natural fact and practice of morality, would have been too much an ivory-tower philosopher's way, not sufficiently in the world. But just what was the use of adding the natural fact and practice to our considerations? As all can see, it is a kind of growth of attitudes somehow relative to place and time, attitudes that conflict among themselves. Their conflict is such that to make a consistent summary of natural morality is necessarily to have settled for a partial one. Why attend to the thing at all?

Then there is the general scepticism about moral utterances that affects nearly all of us, at any rate nearly all readers of books. We are not ever free of the thinking of those who say that moral opinions are personal or subjective, that they consist only in value judgements. Some of us know about Logical Positivism, and its idea that moral judgements are neither true nor false but are merely expressions of emotion. There was also the subsequent Oxford idea, Prescriptivism, that moral judgements are merely imperatives or commands, no nearer to truth than 'Shut the door'. We can take it that there is some similar point in more ordinary stuff. Even in the conceptual mysteriousness of those who allow of something that 'it's right if it's right for you'.

And, to hurry back to philosophy, up-to-date philosophy, we are unlikely to be bowled over by something that wonderfully has taken the name of *Moral Realism*. It seems to say that such a proposition as 'Socialism is right' *can be* just as true and as little subjective as 'Roses are red', or just as false as and no more a matter of personal opinion than 'Roses are green' – because we also make a personal contribution to the existence of colours by way of our eyes and brains. And, finally, and closer to home, we may not be reassured by our own attempts to say more of the truths that have seemed to be at the bottom of morality (p. 36).

I admit to some of these uncertainties, to a weakening of moral confidence about our subject, but they have to come together with something else. Indeed, to be brief, they are made to count for nothing much by something else.

I have in mind the flying of the aeroplanes full of people into the towers, doing that, with further unpredictable results, such as other people jumping out of the towers to their deaths, and then a few months later, more people being torn or burned or suffocated to death by unspeakable bombs and missiles in another place, Afghanistan. Does the wrong of flying the aeroplanes into the towers become *uncertain* when I think of the possibility of my having an excess of empathy, or of some uncertainty about the natural fact and practice of morality, or of morality's being as subjective as it is?

No, I am pleased to say, flying the aeroplanes into the towers does *not* become only uncertainly wrong. There isn't any doubt about it. It is, instead, something whose wrongfulness is real. It was so wrong, as remarked before, that it was something that some American men and women would have killed themselves to prevent.

And what about the 20 million years of living time lost? Those years would have had happy times in them, affection and desire, learning things, some satisfying work, kinds of success, seeing children grow up. Was that loss not really wrong? Is it uncertain that it was wrong that on the day of September 11, if deaths by starvation for the year 2001 were evenly spread throughout it, 24,000 persons died of hunger? Is it just my opinion that that was wrong? No, that wrong was certain and real too. That I have to summon up the facts here, to think, not be confused by the *ordinariness* of the facts – that doesn't make awful deprivation into something doubtful.

So if moral confidence can become less firm, it can also be recovered. It can be recovered, too, by thinking more about the three reasons noticed for giving it up, starting with the one about excessive empathy. Some of us really are bleeding hearts. Maybe I'm one. As for hypocrisy, it exists – some of us do claim to have higher standards or beliefs in our lives than is the case. But neither of those facts does anything at all to the truth that those who have bad lives lack what we claim for ourselves, and that they claim what we must in consistency allow to them. The piece of logic, if as open to replies as almost all pieces of logic, does not work more by empathy or the like, does it, than any other moral claim? Consistency doesn't get its validity and strength from hypocrisy, does it? That doesn't have anything to do with hypocrisy, does it?

So if Nietzsche can make me worry a bit, I can on reflection stand by that three-line biography of him written a while ago, not overly respectful, ending with 'Friend of Wagner, praised by Freud for self-insight, died deranged'. I can and will think some more, not now but sometime, about the role of natural morality in our thinking, and about what will not go away despite the complications, that there are some real truths somewhere about what ought to happen, and our moral responsibility, and our moral standing.

So let us go on to the end with our inquiry.

Our share in September 11

What we have come to in the main so far are two propositions, maybe facts. One is that wrong was done by us by omission in allowing the bad lives, including the almost unthinkable losses of living time. This is so whatever is also to be said of our wrongs by commission as against omission, as in the case of Palestine in particular, but also Iraq and Saudi Arabia. The second proposition is that wrong was done against us on September 11. Let us turn now to something else, recall something else.

To *be* morally responsible for a thing, whether culpably or creditably, is to be a cause of it, a human cause. This moral responsibility is commonly shared. What this comes to is that the thing has several or many causes or conditions, commonly at different times, each of them an act or omission of a person or persons. What it is to be *held* responsible for a thing is to be morally disapproved of or worse, maybe loathed, for the act or omission. Plainly, more than one person can also be held responsible or morally disapproved of for contributing to some effect. The situation is like that in the law, where legal responsibility may be divided between parties, in fact into quantified shares (p. 7).

As for the thing or effect for which you may be responsible or held responsible, that can be another action as well as some other effect. You can be responsible or held responsible for your employee's or subordinate's or someone else's harming of someone.

The second wrong mentioned a moment ago, that of the killers at the Twin Towers, was in some way owed to the first, our omissions with the bad lives. Their wrong was in a way owed to ours. Certainly that does not absolve them. It is indeed a certainty that two wrongs do not make a right. But, to be plainer, the atrocity at the Twin Towers did have a human necessary condition in what preceded it: our deadly treatment of those outside our circle of comfort, those with the bad lives. Without that deadly treatment by us, the atrocity at the Twin Towers would not have happened. As implied a little way back, in connection with the wrong of September 11, our omissions were a necessary context for the particular intentions on the part of the killers having to do with Palestine, Iraq and Saudi Arabia.

Whether or not it can be qualified, it is hard to see how the implicit conclusion can be avoided. It is that we were partly responsible and can be held partly responsible for the 3,000 deaths at the Twin Towers and at the Pentagon. We are rightly to be held responsible along with the killers. We share in the guilt. Those who condemn us have reason to do so. Did we bring the killing at the Twin Towers on ourselves? Did we have it coming? Did we ask for it? Those offensive questions, and their offensive answers *yes*, do contain a truth. We did play a part, our politicians at our head.

For the 3,000 deaths there are lines of responsibility into the past, as real as chains of command, containing earlier and later perpetrators. We in our democracies are in them, and in particular those of us who have got themselves into our governments. We are there with those who aided the killers and with Osama bin Laden. The killers and those who aided them and bin Laden are not alone. We have to escape the long illusion that those of us who are ordinary are innocent.

It seems to me true, if unconventional and not cool, that if there was a proper court for *all* crimes against humanity, Ronald Reagan and Margaret Thatcher in particular would be in it. I guess I mean it. That it will not happen, that in an ordinary sense it is unthinkable, does not entail or even suggest that it ought not to happen. Our conventions do not make moral facts. Our leaders would be there with Slobodan Milosevic, the former President of Yugoslavia and Ariel Sharon of Israel. They wouldn't only be arraigned in their absence in a philosophers' court like the Vietnam War Crimes Tribunal arranged in 1967 in Sweden by my real betters, Jean Paul Sartre and Bertrand Russell.

You may well want to say more about kinds of guilt of persons in the lines of responsibility into the past, and there can be no objection to that sophistication if you have time. I will mainly leave it to you. What you cannot do, as it seems to me, is to give us small parts in the story, put us in the background. We were not just scene-setters. President Bush and Mr Blair and their predecessors were not just scene-setters. It is true, if not the only truth, that we did *immeasurably more* than the killers of September 11, over a greatly longer time. Our contribution to September 11 was no single monstrous act.

Will someone object that this is mad, that we have no responsibility at all, or none to speak of, or little, because the 3,000 killings were the result of the Free Will of those who actually or physically carried them out? Will someone say that we have no *real* responsibility for what others do? No real responsibility for the end of a sequence of events that after our earlier and great part does also have in it the free and responsible decisions and actions of others?

It has been said before, mistakenly. There can be no principle at all for us to depend on in this way. The former President of Yugoslavia *is* on trial in The Hague for deaths and other atrocities physically committed by others. Even if he is in a court of victor's justice, as indeed he is, it is no one's view that he is simply absolved of responsibility by the fact that others pulled the triggers or did the rapes. But we have no need of international law to establish what we all accept in all contexts excepting those where we stand accused ourselves. If I destroy your family by attack or fraud or victimization, and you attack me, I bear a responsibility for my wounds. I have brought them on myself.

Some will want, as before, to draw attention to the fact that the killings of September 11, whatever else is true of them, were a response to particular grievances. They were, as Osama bin Laden said, responses to what has happened and is happening in Palestine, Iraq and Saudi Arabia. Do you want to dispute what was said by me about a necessary context for these grievances, the context of a world of bad lives? Do you want to say that if there can be terrorism for humanity, what happened on September 11 was not it? Let us, if necessary, agree to differ. There is something else that does not depend on agreement and will remain true. It is quite enough for certain further purposes of mine, which, incidentally, do not include self-mortification.

Think along the same lines as before (p. 120). Think of acts of terrorism on the scale of September 11 but with the clear and known goal of the principle of humanity. Think if you want of an attack on another great American symbol. The goal of it is the saving of people from bad lives wherever they are, those who are worst-off first. Those Africans. However the goal is articulated, it has the fundamental strength of the principle of humanity.

If there were such an attack tomorrow, it would be wrong. It would be wrong because it would be irrational. That is, it could not be judged that in this world as it is, the world of our democracies, it would succeed in its goal. It could not be judged that it would go in some significant way or degree to serve that goal.

What is also true is that we, most of all our democratic governments and those of us most in control of them from outside, would share in the moral responsibility for the atrocity. We would have a responsibility unmitigated by any hesitation you suppose to be in place with respect to the goal of the actual terrorism of September 11. It would be untouched by any hesitancy about Iraq or Saudi Arabia. If you take the view, for example, that Islamic terrorism is insufficiently impartial, there would be no such complication, or less such complication, in the contemplated terrorism for humanity.

What is in question here is not just a possible responsibility. What is in question is not just a responsibility for an imagined act, a responsibility that we would have if something were to happen. What we have here is a conclusion about actuality, about what we have done and what we are. We have done what and we are what would give us a responsibility, yet clearer than in the case of September 11, for another hideous and monstrous act. Whether or not such an act is ever performed, we *are* now such that it could be laid at our door as well as the door of others. We would have asked for it. We would again be earlier as against later perpetrators.

Having recovered my moral confidence, at least for a minute or two, I bring myself to add something else, something worse, with the same further purpose. That purpose is not to harrow you or me, but to try to have a full sense of ourselves, and also of urgency in the matter of what needs to be done. What is to be added, which is of a piece with what we have, has to do with September 11, as I think, and yet more certainly with the speculation as to other possible or conceivable terrorism, terrorism for humanity.

We have it, to speak too mildly, that September 11 was wrong and the other terrorism would be wrong. One was and one would be wrong because of irrationality. September 11 was wrong because it could not be judged as likely to succeed in its goal. Should you wish to reduce the requirement to the one sometimes mentioned in connection with a just war, the requirement of a reasonable hope, that will not help. There was not *a reasonable hope* with the Twin Towers. There would not be a reasonable hope, in our world today, for the terrorism for humanity.

What if our world and we had been in a way different before September 11? What if that horror could have had more than a reasonable hope of success? What if we were different, more open to reflection, including self-reflection, less subject to an illusion of moral reality? In a word, what if that horror had been rational? If we do what is not easy, and requires some fortitude, which is to hold in mind the bad lives, the sample loss of 20 million years of living time, does a conclusion follow? Does the conclusion follow that the rational horror would have been right? What about that other conceivable terrorism with another goal, terrorism for humanity?

Well, I have not enough fortitude for more of this and leave the matter to you. It could be that the question should not be contemplated, for fear of making wrongful terror more likely. Even if we do not follow such a principle of caution at all in connection with our wars. Anyway, I leave the question. It is enough for my further purpose that it exists.

Capitalism

To come now to our counter-attack against Islamic terrorism after September 11, and then to the last matter, what is to be done, it will be useful or necessary to look again at ourselves. It will be useful in the one case and necessary in the other to do what we kept on putting off – think about another whole side of our way of life. If this side of our life has entered into feelings about the counter-attack, and is fundamental to the question of what is to be done, it bears as well on conclusions drawn already. Whatever we come to think of ourselves in this way will throw a light backwards as well as forwards.

In connection with the original attack on September 11, the possibility that it was wrong because it was against democracy was considered and excluded. We did not look into the braver idea that the attack was wrong because it was against the complementary half of our way of life is not political, not the fact of our democracy. That other half, certainly connected, is economic rather than political. What it comes to is what was once disdained and then tolerated as *capitalism*, and now is more likely to be approved of or celebrated by those who use the name. What I have in mind also goes under the less distracting and anodyne names of *big business* and just *business*.

Do you think it odd to look at ourselves as capitalists in connection with the question of whether it was wrong of them to attack us and right of us to counter-attack them? Admittedly *Time* magazine has not quite offered us the argument 'We are capitalists, therefore it is OK for us to bomb Afghanistan'. Is it not true, however, that a good many of us had the attitude that we are reasonable, enlightened and indeed advanced societies, and so we are unlikely to be making a real mistake in any counter-attack? Americans certainly felt that. So it will be at least useful to contemplate the business side of our societies, that side of what we are now taught to know as our *civilization*.

You may want to dig in your heels against this line of thought. You may suppose that with the question of the counter-attack we ought to be concerned, rather, with something like the principles of *the just war*. Maybe whether we had *just cause* to bomb Afghanistan and whether we did so with discrimination and proportion?

Well, I certainly see the point of that kind of reflection, but it doesn't preoccupy me. To my mind that kind of reflection is a little like the tail of the dog, not the dog. What really gives us confidence in international conflicts is being in the right, where in part that is being a person or society generally on morally higher ground than another, or at least generally on somehow more reasonable or advanced ground. Judgements of international justice rest on rather than form the basis of such judgements of standing. We go along with the judgements of international justice when they seem to us to be right, and we ignore them, if we can, when they seem wrong.

Americans with good memories or who read an occasional good book will remember that Nicaragua took Mr Reagan's America to the World Court for America's proxy and other attacks on it in the 1980s – those attacks that fall pretty squarely under a lot of definitions of terrorism, including our own. The World Court found America guilty, and America told the World Court where to go. It told the Security Council of the United Nations too, and the General Assembly.

So we should look at our economic system or remind ourselves about it in connection with what we did in Afghanistan. The other reason for looking at our economic system is larger. With respect to the question of what to do now, there is the idea that what we need to do, for our safety, is to make the rest of the world more like us. What we need to do is to export America. We need what we have learned to call globalization, more precisely a global transition to our economic system. That will make everything OK, or anyway closer.

There is a still larger side to this consideration. The question of what is to be done is not just the question of what is to be done about terrorism. It is the question of what is to be done as a result of the thinking about ourselves to which the terrorism of September 11 gave rise. It wasn't all prudential or self-concerned thinking, all about our safety and security.

Do you say September 11 did not and ought not to have given rise to any self-reflection? Do you declare with the injured innocence of Mr Rumsfeld, the Secretary of Defence, that the United States is not and never has been a problem? Seemingly no part of any problem? Well, I have the idea that September 11 *did* give rise to self-reflection, and still does, on the part of quite a few of us, and anyway that it ought to have and still ought to – a lot of this reflection being about our economic system. Have a look at it with me.

It has as much to do as our democracy with our means to our shared end, the great goods, and it is therefore of as great an importance. The great goods, you will remember, are longer lives, a certain quality of life, freedom and power and safety, respect and self-respect, human relationships, and the satisfactions of cultures, the last including not only art but also education, religion, and recreation.

It would be wrong to regard all the means to these things as material. The happy poor, taken as people not extremely or appallingly deprived, do exist (p. 22). So do the unhappy rich, some of them unhappy because of being short on respect, relationships, or satisfactions in the several sides of culture. Still, if not all the means to the great goods are material, it is safe to say that the material means are the main ones. For a start, they are as good as sufficient for longer lives and for the mentioned quality of life, and they have been more or less fundamental to freedom and power. Certainly they play large parts in the other three great goods.

Within material means are *means of production and exchange*, understood in a wide sense to include not only such things as farms, factories, stock markets, trade-names and department stores, but also such things as roads, airspace, energy supplies, and means of settling disputes. These are means to means – means to the existence and possession of personal and immediate means to a good life, such things as apartments, food, medicines, cars, clothes, entertainment and so on. The means of production and exchange have divided into privately-owned and publicly-owned ones, along with hybrids. The privately-owned ones are *capital* in the relevant sense of the term.

Capitalism or business, the privately-owned system of producing and distributing personal means to well-being, is a system in which the private owners take profits from the system as well as pay themselves if they work in it. The others who work in it receive no profits, only pay or wages. It is also of importance that the owners and their executives have greater control than those who run publicly-owned means of production and exchange. They are less subject to governments and voters.

They have this greater control over the purchase of raw materials, the pay of workers, the supply and price of products, and, very crucially, the amount of profits and pay taken by themselves. This fact of their system has no counterpart with respect to publicly-owned production and exchange. Although capitalism or business so described includes local garages, dry cleaners, grocery stores and delicatessens, it is the corporations, international traders and media empires that are in several ways most important.

It is integral to capitalism that what is produced by the joint efforts of owners and workers, taking into account the efforts of the owners who do work, is distributed by way of a market. The exchanging of goods by buying and selling. Here there is some competition and also some collaboration among the sellers. The market to some extent determines what is produced and supplied. Buyers or customers demand products and services, and capitalists supply the products and the raw materials that go into them.

What to say of it all? It is not difficult to be more confident here. Not much fortitude is required.

The exchanging of goods between people is about as natural a thing in human existence as there is, and the same can be said of using money in it. Each of us is likely to have something of value, if only the results of our muscles, in whose place we would prefer to have something else. You've bought this book, I hope.

But it is as natural to suppose that there should be things that are not bought and sold. One is national defence and another is babies. It would be dangerous for national defence to be in private hands, and the general selling of babies would not be good for the babies. It doesn't seem quite the thing, either, that you should only have as much protection against rape as you can pay for. Not everything should be privatized.

Also, with respect to the exchanging of goods, if all a man gets to support his family is to come from the labour market, and what it will pay him is too little to feed them, is that OK? It has been natural for most of us to suppose that there should be some control on amounts of things exchanged, rates of exchange, for example the pay of workers for their work. In civilized societies, as conceived by some in the past, there is a decent minimum wage.

From these thoughts and others, and also recent and earlier history, it is clear that capitalism or business as we have quickly sketched it actually covers a range of things. A little or a lot can be left to publicly-owned means of production and exchange. Energy supplies can be a matter of public utilities or not. So with railways. There can be more or less regulation of pay, working conditions, and so on. There can certainly be market-socialism, which keeps a market but reduces the private ownership.

Let us then have in mind the actual system we are taking forward with us in the new millennium. The actual version or model we have of the sort of thing sketched. Think of business in America, Canada, Britain, France, Germany, Italy, Spain, Denmark and Japan in about 2003. Think of that system that is entirely bound up with the inequalities of income and wealth in our societies already noticed several times. Such as Americans of the top tenth having seventeen times the income of the bottom tenth, and a few thousand times the wealth of the bottom four tenths (pp. 8, 111, 113).

There are very many arguments offered for this kind and degree of capitalism that we have. One batch of arguments, with a natural beginning, has to do with efficiency and indeed rationality. It is clear that my exchanging things with you can be an effective and economical means to my current ends. The conservative economist Friedrich Hayek, sometimes taken as a part-time philosopher, also had a thought of some value when he stressed the market can be a kind of ordering mechanism – a way of calling up what people want. That thought may have been better than his other one, when Russia was Russia, to the effect that if we don't have all-out capitalism, the great bear will come along and eat us up.

At a lower level, but still to do with efficiency, there is a large difference made between people who get a profit and people who don't. Or more particularly, there is a large difference made between an organization with the former category of persons in it and other organizations. Since they can give themselves a lot more money if they work very hard, we are told, they work very hard. Free-enterprisers and their employees work harder than public servants, and get your parcel there on time. They are persons of entrepreneurial zest, realism in place of conventionality, executive drive, and so on. The pursuit of profit gives us these blessings.

Another whole batch of arguments for our capitalism has to do with freedom, or rather freedoms. There is the thought, first of all, that our exchanging things, selling and buying in a market, is itself a freedom of the very greatest importance. Free enterprise. That is to say, in part, that making a profit is such a freedom. It has been supposed that necessarily there is greater choice offered to ordinary people in more capitalist societies. It has been supposed, often, on the assumption that privately-owned as against publicly-owned or cooperative enterprises are more efficient, that the former are better producers of any freedom in particular, say freedom to travel.

It has often been supposed there is more to be said of capitalism and freedom. There is the defence of capitalism that there is a connection between it and democracy, or some capitalism in particular and some democracy in particular. It used to be added, too, that without the power of private wealth in a society, or now the great power of the corporations, there would be more dictators and tyrants, not to mention great bears of societies.

Thirdly, after efficiency and freedom, there is also a very mixed bag of arguments. 1. Our business and international business is the natural result of a seed so natural as to be *human*. That is private property. Each of us wants his own toothbrush for a start. 2. Business or capitalism is what is best for any society, as proved by the Cold War between us and the Russians. We won. 3. In the past, capitalism has produced an ever-increasing supply of the means to the great goods. Nothing else could or would have. 4. The gifted persons in it, already noted, do not just produce and deliver well, but are of a general value to society, say in government. Burke used to go on about a natural aristocracy. 5. Individual capitalists, if they work in their enterprises, deserve their profits for their longer hours or the like, and those who do not actually work deserve their profits for risking their capital for the common good. 6. Advertising creatively enriches our cultures, including street-life.

Fourthly and finally, there are some recommendations or anyway announcements to the effect that our capitalism has some very general worth that sums it all up. One is that it is part and parcel of the free society, which is somehow a larger fact than just democracy. Another, of which you heard earlier in connection with Adam Smith, is that capitalism is the system called for by Utilitarianism, the principle that we are to go for what produces the greatest total of satisfaction – there is a hidden hand that brings it about that if each of us seeks his own advantage, that will make everything work out for the best, or anyway the greatest happiness. Another more technical general recommendation is attached to the name of the Italian economist Wilfredo Pareto. This is that when our market works perfectly, and we get to a point where all the free exchanges have been made, any further change has to take something away from somebody who wants it, reduce somebody's well-being.

So there are four bundles of stuff on one side of a debate that still goes on to some extent between political parties and in the papers

135

and on our screens. To come to a main question, a general and large question that can indeed be asked, how good is that whole side of the argument for our capitalism or our business system as we have it? What are the recommendations or arguments worth? You can get bogged down in one or another of them, but for certain purposes there is no need. You can ask the general question.

In America, there are not just those differences of income and wealth, but also what goes with them. To recall the fact to your attention, you die a lot earlier if you are a black. You still die a lot earlier despite whatever recent improvement in race relations comes to mind. In England and Wales you die earlier if you have no skills, which you may well have been entirely unable to acquire. In both places, if you are towards the bottom of the pile, you are deprived to different extents the other things we all want – material well-being, freedom and the like, respect and self-respect, the goods of relationship, and culture. In short, you have the life of a lesser creature. The inequality is getting worse, not better. A lot of theory about capitalism forgets there are soup kitchens in America, that they are not a fact of the Depression of the 1930s, and that a quarter of pre-school children live in poverty. The facts are in different ways similar in Britain, Canada, France, Germany, Italy, Spain, Japan and like places. Denmark is better.

If you will allow me to remind you again of the rest of the world outside our circle, there are the half-lives, and the children dying before five, and the quarter-lives, and the sample of 20 million years of life lost. There is the wider fact of vicious deprivation of goods other than a decent length of life. Asthma is pretty bad if you've had it, but asthma with no medication to control it is different. It is not *living* that goes on at the bottom in Malawi, Mozambique, Zambia or Sierra Leone, only something less. There is also the example of Palestine.

It would take either a dimwit or a monster of ideology to think of this world as other than a world of bad lives. It would surely take such a person, too, to think it could not have been otherwise, and that it could not be otherwise in the future. If you are tempted to that supposed realism, think of our past war efforts. You do not need to be an intuitive or reflective supporter of the principle of humanity, or curiously hopeful about possibilities, to know this is a world of bad lives and that it could have been and could be different.

It is a world owed about as much to our capitalism or business as to our hierarchic democracy. Our capitalism as we have it is one of two engines of this world. Something seems to me to follow from that, the main proposition here. It seems to follow that the four batches of recommendations or arguments for our capitalism are worth about *nothing*. That is the value assigned to them by somebody outside our circle of comfort and hungry and with his or her head screwed on. That value looks to me correct. It is the value put on the batches by the principle of humanity. Is it not the value put on the batches by the natural fact and practice of morality when it is not being managed for purposes of profit?

The matter can be put differently, in terms of the kind of argument known as *reductio ad absurdum*. That is an argument that shows that some premise or set of premises must be mistaken because they issue in a conclusion that is absurd. Formal logicians require that the conclusion be a self-contradiction, but nobody else does. The particular *reductio ad absurdum* we seem to have is that a lot of arguments issue in the conclusion that the world is OK, maybe as good as possible. That conclusion is absurd. So the arguments must be mistaken, to say the least.

Do you say you've paid for the book and so let's have some comment on particular arguments in the four batches? Those that aren't immediately vulnerable themselves to the *reductio ad absurdum*? You will have to make do with only a little of what strikes me as unnecessary. Readers like short books, and authors like readers to finish books.

It is surely only political economists, by which I mean economists on a political mission, who can think that there is any important sense at all in which the business system we have is more efficient than alternative business or market systems. If there are two ways of getting some valuable thing, some large means to well-being, and the second way involves not only the costs of getting it, including good pay and salaries for those who provide it, but also profits of millions or billions of dollars or pounds, then before anything else is said, the second way is patently and tremendously less efficient. While Afghanistan has been being reported, much of the British press has also had in it the bonuses and golden handshakes creamed off the top of industries. It is not *efficient* for us to run something in order to make immense profits when it could be run at least as well for a lot less.

No doubt some bureaucracies are impediments, but can anyone who really thinks about the losses to a society of not having more of a common plan, of duplication of effort, waste, depletion of resources, the cost of a lot of things being more the result of advertising them than of what's in them and making them, and so on, really think we're *efficient*?

As for Pareto, suppose our market system is working perfectly, which it isn't in sight of doing. All the free exchanges have been made for the moment, and so any further change would take something away from somebody who wants it, reduce somebody's well-being. Just for a start, this situation is perfectly consistent with appalling destruction of the environment and whatever else. It is perfectly consistent with people dying of starvation in the streets. Efficiency is supposed to give us something better than this, isn't it, supposed to serve some decent end?

Many untheoretical persons in England, Scotland and Wales, by the way, know about the matter of efficiency on the basis of personal experience, a small litmus test touched on earlier. British Rail, the publicly-owned system, used to be made political fun of by newspapers on a mission because trains were late when the public servants couldn't get the wrong kind of snow or the wrong kind of leaves off the tracks. That has changed.

Now that the system has been profitized, turned into a few dozen pieces of private enterprise, the snow and leaves still stay on the tracks but the trains come off. People die because of the lack of improvements in safety that could have been paid for by what is now taken in private profit. The trains are late not just because of the snow and the leaves, but late all the time. The prices of tickets, as compared with other European railways, are extraordinary, a bad dream that is real. Everybody knows that the result of this small litmus test for privatization is disaster, except my New Labour government. And, I hear by email, American newspapers in favour of some more American privatization of Amtrak.

To come to the batch of arguments about freedom, it is easy to use an argument having to do with freedom for anything whatever that can come into the mind of someone in or out of political power. Of *every* political party and movement there ever was, it is true that it offered and proclaimed some freedom. It offered to remove some obstacle or impediment to some desire. Some parties and movements offered a society the possibility of being free of some minority within it, and when in power freed the society by killing the minority. There are personal, social, political, cultural and other freedoms. There is no mistake, but only a habit of language, that stands in the way of speaking of a freedom to live a full length of life.

Thus, in short, to defend business or capitalism as a system that provides a freedom or freedoms is at best to begin an argument, one which will have to say rather more about losses of freedoms. The only way of taking the argument forward, given the welter of considerations to and fro, freedoms gained and freedoms lost, is to have some higher principle that assigns weight or importance to each particular one. You will know what principle I depend on. The principle of humanity, for a start, assigns lesser importance to the freedom of shareholders and greater importance to all of us having a decent life. It assigns the greatest importance to what we can indeed call freedoms of six fundamental kinds, freedoms to have the six great goods.

In contrast, what general principle can be used to defend our capitalism as we have it? Or anyway, what sums it up? What explains why it has the particular features that it does have? Some people, having been reading the English papers about the profits, bonuses and golden handshakes, say that the principle is selfishness. Greed is the creed, they say. What explains our capitalism is an extraordinary degree of selfishness. But saying this misses the point, or does not put it well. I used to know some socialists, before the breed went into hiding, and they were not pure altruists. Some had swimming pools.

The difference between our capitalists and the rest of us, or so I concluded a while ago, is not that we are not selfish and they are. The difference is that some of us are self-interested and also have a moral principle, such as the one about humanity, but the business persons are self-interested and seem to have no general *moral* principle at all. Nothing that is true to the basic stuff in the natural fact and practice of morality. They look to me to have no underlying principle of a recognizably moral kind, but only bits and pieces of stuff in various batches that cannot really stand examination.

So much for a view of the economic as against the political side of our societies. The sides are tied together, certainly, and strengthen one another. There is an awful lot of overlap between capitalism in its board rooms and that interest-group of the top tenth that has a dominance in the hierarchies of our democracies (p. 113). Is it unfair of me to mention in passing what to a European is a ludicrous fact? Well, it's a fact, and how much less ludicrous is it than some others? It's just that New York's new mayor, Mr Bloomberg, got elected by personally spending $68,968,185 on the election – $92.60 for each vote he got. The unsuccessful Mr Green's campaign cost about $16,500,000. I don't think the Humanity Party would have got much of a look-in.

But leave all that. My critical view of our economic arrangements, to stick to that, is one with which you may or may not agree, but it is one you will have to contemplate. The *reductio ad absurdum* will not go away. Keeping the critical view in mind will also be rational in another way, not intellectually. There are a lot of people, a few of them with bombs, who are of my mind. There are more people in the world of my mind than of any other, aren't there?

Our counter-attack

One conclusion to be drawn from this interlude can be drawn quickly. In the welter of feelings and arguments for and against our counter-attack on Islamic terrorism, one can be discarded. We could not and cannot draw confidence in this counter-attack from our system for providing ourselves and others with the means to the great goods. More particularly, we cannot reassure ourselves by a feeling of moral or other reasonableness with respect to our capitalism – those material means to the great goods having to do with production and exchange.

Among other thoughts as to sources of confidence for our counter-attack, one looks back to a possibility we considered about the attack on the Twin Towers and the Pentagon. That possibility was that the attack was wrong because it was an attack against democracy. On reflection, it seemed hard to give a lot of weight to that, given that our democracy is hierarchic democracy. The situation is the same with the thought now that we can have a confidence in our counter-attack that is owed to its source in democracy. We cannot have such a confidence, whatever else is to be said. Our democracy no more recommends the bombing of Afghanistan than does our other arrangement with respect to the great goods, our economic arrangement.

The counter-attack was not made right, either, by something that in fact was part of it and turns up in some thinking on the general subject of punishment. There is an understanding of a theory of punishment in terms of desert or retribution that is unusual in that it makes some clear sense of talk of desert. Here, the idea is not to try to justify the imprisoning or executing of a man by only a past fact, which is more mystery-morality. What the idea comes to, when made explicit, is the attempt to justify the thing by the *satisfaction* it gives to victims and others for the past wrong. Punishment is taken as legally-arranged revenge.

That this is clear does not make it tolerable. No man is rightly executed or imprisoned for the reason that this retribution satisfies a grievance, reduces or ends a bitterness. The gain cannot conceivably justify the loss. Americans, or at any rate a number of their journalists, wanted retribution and revenge after September 11. They couldn't thereby have a justification for action. You cannot tear people apart or burn or choke them to death for reasons of just *feeling*, reasons of national satisfaction. That is not civilization but barbarism.

So there are some things that cannot give us justification or confidence in our counter-attack. It is as true, to look back some more to our earlier reflections, that certain thoughts in the opposite direction, inclinations to condemn rather than justify our counter-attack, do not really work either.

One earlier conclusion was that we do certainly bear a responsibility for the great wrong of bad lives, for our omissions in this respect and also for our positive actions or commissions (pp. 85–6). The omissions and commissions, as can now incidentally be added, are carried out by our hierarchic democracies and our capitalism, in particular our international capitalism. That the omissions and commissions have these sources tells us more about them, throws them into another light, but forget about that. A second earlier conclusion was that we also share responsibility for the wrong of the killings of September 11.

No doubt there are Islamic moralists who will draw their own further conclusion from these two wrongs and the responsibilities for them – that we can claim no moral ground for our counter-attack. That is not my view, and I hope that by now it is not yours. It is results that matter. We did not have clean hands when we sent our own killers to Afghanistan, but that in itself does not condemn us. If the only defensible actions were by people with clean hands, there would be rather fewer of them.

As you will gather, what I have in mind in thinking about our attack on Afghanistan is the consequentialist morality of humanity. Like any other morality that can be made explicit and claims attention, it is not mysterious, and in particular it is not mysterious about the past. It attends to the good and bad that can come of actions. It is a possibility to be considered, certainly, that good and the avoidance of bad justified our use of our dirty hands in Afghanistan.

You can persist in thinking of the possibility despite a good deal else. Our response to September 11 was not only about reducing the chance of bad things, but a defence of our Western power in economics and politics. It was also a war of the strong against the weak, the rich against the poor, the mostly safe against the vulnerable. Was there much honour in past wars? There was not much of it in Afghanistan in killing boys in pick-up trucks from a height of 15,000 feet. It wasn't killing in cowardice, I suppose, but certainly killing in comfort. Live in comfort and kill in comfort.

Our responsibility, and what to do

The Times of London one day carried on its front page a picture and story of a smiling and chubby 26-year-old on the deck of the aircraft carrier *USS Carl Vinson*. She was in her F14 Tomcat, a jet suited to dropping the precision-guided bombs. She had spent some of her childhood in England and so her American accent was impure. The heading was 'Action woman Mumbles flies into heat of battle'. She said she'd always had her heart set on being a fighter pilot, and was just doing her job in Afghanistan.

She was different, certainly, from those men who flew their victims into the Twin Towers. Was she repulsive and inhuman? Not at all. Jolly, rather, and maybe a little shy. Did we readers think of identifying in a bodily way with those people dismembered or fried by her bombs? Few of us did. Since we did not have such feelings, were we disqualified from thinking about war? I guess not. But you could take time, sometime, to think more on the matter and the comparison with the other killers. You could think some more, I guess, about that fifth part of ordinary morality (p. 90).

As for now, let us persist in thinking about whether our counterattack on Afghanistan was justified by a good judgement as to its good consequences. Or could it be that there is an escape from turning over the question – an escape in the idea that nothing else was actually possible? We do not have to turn over reasons, pro and con, for the rightness of bombing Afghanistan if nothing else was possible. As philosophers used to say, 'ought' implies 'can'. You are only under a moral obligation to do what you are able to do – you can't be held morally responsible for something if you couldn't have done otherwise. You can't be held to account for not stopping the burglars leaving with the silver if you were tied up in the corner.

Is it possible to extrapolate from such simple examples to something else, where the impossibility is a matter of human nature rather than physical constraint or force? No one expected, after September 11, that there would be no response in kind. Did some of us think that doing nothing was *impossible* – meaning just that, actually or humanly impossible, as against its being morally impossible to do nothing, where that just means it would be absolutely wrong to do nothing? Well, it did feel a little bit like that.

143

You could think, if you were like me, that the best thing that could happen would be for us all to wake up, hear that terrible moral alarm clock of September 11, and start changing some bad lives. Only that and nothing else. That is what would happen in a better world. But what went along with that was the other idea, that in this world as it is, maybe, the Americans in a non-moral sense had to do something about September 11. There wasn't, maybe, any other actual or human possibility.

If we now took some time with this question, we might conclude that 'ought' implies 'can' has to have something more complicated put in its place. Part of it is that moral disapproval or condemnation for something is a matter of degree, and it varies along with the degree of possibility that there was of not doing the thing. To put it another way, moral disapproval or condemnation for something is the less according to how humanly difficult or how near to impossible it was to do something else. In my opinion, again not so confident, there *is* something to be said along these lines about the counter-attack. Mr Bush and his administration did not have a lot of leeway – real or human as against moral leeway.

But that is not to exclude the moral question. It is still there. It still needs an answer. To the extent that we could, an extent that existed, were we right to come together and counter-attack?

It was my feeling that a counter-attack had to be judged to be a way of reducing the probability of more attacks like September 11, more such horrors. The balance of judgement had to be that a counter-attack would make more September 11s less likely, and not lead to other disaster. It would not lead to more war, more state-terrorism, and more of other terrorism.

In passing let me mention an idea that has been creeping up. Is morality itself a difficult matter? Is it very hard to figure out the right principle or principles? It doesn't seem as hard as something else, which is judging facts, in particular judging the probability of consequences, trying to see what will flow from an action or course of action, in the long run certainly but also in the short run. What makes it hard to see the right thing is not so much seeing, according to me, the moral truth of the principle of humanity. What makes it hard is seeing how the world will work out.

If bombing Afghanistan could be taken as likely to lessen the chance of more Islamic attacks on us without the other possible effects mentioned, it could not conceivably be our only right response to September 11. In all of life, from bedrooms and kitchens to hemi-spheres of the globe, we learn of the distress of others, after words have failed to teach us, from their actions, or from actions by others on their behalf. We learned or could have learned something from the attack on the Twin Towers. Or, we did or could have realized something more fully. We could have come to an actual realization of our actual responsibility for the bad lives, and also for that same attack of September 11.

We were required by September 11, in my view, to see ourselves and reform ourselves. More than that, a confession was called for, and a resolution of change. Are you so worldly as to suppose talk of *confession* is unrealistic and a matter of religion at best? I have a sense of your possible reasons, but I do not agree. Confession is possible. Countries and peoples have confessed before now. Germany did. There is also confession to oneself, in private. A people can do it. It is something important for the future rather than the past.

To come now to a first actual conclusion about the right or wrong of our counter-attack, it is that if it was conjoined with self-perception and resolution to change, it was defensible. A second actual conclusion is that if it was not accompanied by the better thing, it was not defensible. It was wrong. In the absence of self-perception, indeed some kind of resolution of change, the counter-attack was wrong independently of the pieces of horror properly reported by a few honest and effective journalists, the public mistreat-ment and humiliation of prisoners as a further threat, the violations of the Geneva Convention certified by the Red Cross, and so on.

There is a particular reason for the conclusion that if the counter-attack was our only response to September 11, it was wrong. In short it is that the counter-attack by itself, unaccompanied by self-perception, would strengthen a side of our societies. It would strengthen that side, including almost all of those on top in our societies, whose desire or inclination it is to have things go on as before. Unreflectively to engage in and win a battle is almost certainly to fall into a conviction of rectitude. Did our winning the Cold war not prove our moral superiority? In a way, of course, that a victory by Hitler early in that war would not have proved his. Victory alone in Afghanistan could lead to more war by us. It could lead to a wrongful war on Iraq. It would certainly have the effect of reinforcing our political and economic systems.

You will have noticed, reader, that the sentences expressing the two conclusions have been chosen with a purpose. They are conditional sentences, with 'if's in them. They do not say whether we learned or not from September 11. They do not say whether our counter-attack did in fact have the accompaniment of self-perception and resolution that would make it morally tolerable. In fact, I do not know. It is not easy to tell. It is not a simple matter. The Commentary page of the *International Herald Tribune* has had on it a variety of pieces, by somewhat different sorts of Americans, sharing the message that America needs not only to bomb but to learn. There was one about a global minimum wage.

It will take time to see what has happened. It will take time before the two conditional conclusions above can be used to arrive at another one, a categorical conclusion about the counter-attack, about whether it was on the side of humanity. It may be that we have to remain in doubt for a good while. I doubt the rightness of the attack myself. It seems likely that the *Herald Tribune* has published good intentions before. Figures about wealth and income, and dying early and the rest, have survived embarrassments before now.

Do you smell a cop-out? You did indeed hear earlier that what it is right to do on any occasion is what will turn out for the best according to the best available information and judgement. What it is right to do, according to me, is what will reduce the bad lives rather than increase them, according to the best available information and judgement. So there will always *be* an answer as to what to do, even if the best available information is uncertain. So each of us can always be asked for an answer beforehand as to what ought to be done. I still say that. So there is a right answer already. My problem is that I don't see it. I've got a bad feeling but not a real answer to the question about the counter-attack. I don't see America and the rest of us clearly enough to have one. Do you?

What is to be done

The last question with which we will be concerned is that of what we need to do. It is asked when our killing in Afghanistan is over, and Pakistan and India remain at peace, but when even the immediate future in all the world is uncertain. There can be more Islamic terrorism, maybe worse. Israel can make still more use of September 11. There can be war. There can be war led by America against Iraq. An answer to the question of what to do can be made nonetheless, one that follows from what at least I have been able to come to believe and feel.

We need to change the world of bad lives, and not just to make more terrorism against us less likely. The first is our greatest obligation, but it is fortunate that the two things go together. We, Americans first among us, have the main obligation to change the world. This follows from the fact of power and the fact that we have had by far the largest part in bringing the world we have into being. But what means are we to try to use?

Leaving for a while the question of particular means, there is a question of a general means, a general policy. It cannot possibly be that our policy should be the exporting of our hierarchic democracy and our capitalism as we have them. On the contrary, we need to try to raise up our societies. Our societies as they are, if you will put up with some last plain speaking, are ignorant, stupid, selfish, managed and deceived for gain, self-deceived, and deadly.

The percentage of people in our societies who have what you could call knowledge rather than an ignorant inkling of the facts in this book, for example, the average life-expectancies in the four African countries, is minuscule. The percentage who have some knowledge of our commissions as distinct from our omissions, although they have not been our main concern, is also minuscule. Hardly any of us knows of the extent of what has been practised by

147

the United States in the past quarter-century and certainly falls under our ordinary definition of state-terrorism. There is ignorance, too, of the nature of our democracies and our capitalism.

The stupidity of our societies is not a condition of mind owed to inheritance or nature. It is rather a condition of mind, a low capability of judgement, that is a consequence of the ignorance. That ignorance, to revert to it, is itself partly a consequence of there being so little of what deserves the name of education or of learning inside or outside of schools and universities. The ignorance is partly a consequence, too, of a society whose public information, by way of most television and such newspapers as Mr Murdoch's, is dismally partial. It is a consequence too of leaders, sometimes false to their political traditions, who make no real attempt to rise above unthinking conventions of use to them, and habits of thought of captains of industry and the like by whom they are too impressed.

The first of the propositions of this stupidity is that you can always get out of things – you can always make a distinction between yourself and others that serves your purpose or your view of things. You can do it explicitly and implicitly. Those killed on your side are individuals, sons and fathers, who would have been doing something this weekend. That is right, but it does not go well with your taking the dead on the other side to be just numbers. There are more consequential inconsistencies, of course. Other propositions of our stupidity, as you will anticipate, have to do with toleration or worse of our societies themselves.

The selfishness, to come to that, is made explicit in the columns of that table of figures with which we started (p. 8) and in many other ways. Much of the selfishness comes from ignorance and stupidity. A lot of it comes from the large fact of our capitalism that is the advertising industry. The deceptions of advertising, its merely self-serving use of what truth it contains, do not conceal its essential nature. That is to call up and reinforce self-interest, to raise and shape self-interested or merely personal desires. Those who work in the agencies, capable of speaking of their creativity, could usefully descend to looking at the figures in the table and thinking about their creative contribution to them.

The question of the management and deception of our societies by those at the top of them is one whose answers are typically effects of that control. In thinking of the management and deception of our cultures, is some Thrasymachean savagery in order? A little attention to the idea that not only justice is what is in the interest of those on top, but also a good deal of what passes as sense and rationality? Better, say I, to err on the side of Thrasymachus than to be cozened into giving up an actual sight of things, without the drapery, because someone says it is conspiracy theory.

It is not only deceived cultures that we have, of course, but also self-deceiving ones. Self-deception is not successfully lying to yourself, your being two minds, one of which does not know the other one. Self-deception is staying in a state of uncertainty about something, keeping a question open and unanswered. Better no answer than one you may get. The way to do this is to keep away from places where you will get an answer, stay away from the evidence. We do this a lot. It is another part of the stupidity of our cultures.

Our leaders come to mind yet again. Mine comes to my mind. So does the idea of something related to a self-contradiction – an inconsistent triad, which is a set of three propositions not all of which can be true.

Mr Blair is not good at plain-speaking, as his God knows. Still, there is the first proposition that his words often sound a real note of moral concern, sometimes about the poor in Africa. There was that moving speech to a New Labour Party conference. The second proposition is that he hasn't actually done anything along those lines, anywhere. To start at home, before you get to Africa, and as you have heard already, the gap between the rich and the poor as officially defined was widening under the previous administration. That was a grim summary of the badness in England. The rich getting richer and the poor getting poorer. This hasn't stopped under Mr Blair's administration. It's gone right on. The third proposition is that Mr Blair seems not actually a hypocrite, but a decent enough bloke, not somebody who knowingly claims he has higher standards and feelings than he does.

All three propositions can't be true, can they? One idea for dealing with them involves amending the third one. If Mr Blair is not a hypocrite, he may be good at self-deception. Really good. Maybe he doesn't really take in what he himself talks about. Maybe he is the leader we deserve, the leader perfectly suited to a culture of self-deception. If the state of self-deception is not exactly the state of hypocrisy, it is open to a lot of question and can be culpable.

The ignorance, stupidity, selfishness, management and deception, and self-deception of our societies are sources of their deadliness. We do what I hope some future century will look back on as hellish things. Larger hellish things than the slave-trade we look back on. These things are like what has prompted all this thinking, September 11. They too, when you come to see them, are hideous and monstrous.

What remains is the matter of more particular means, political means and personal ones, towards the end of changing ourselves in order to change the world of bad lives.

Our own record of persistence with the bad lives raises the question in a mind or two of terrorism by some of ourselves against ourselves. It comes up in Italy. Our betters, say the one or two, will only learn that way. September 11 taught something to those who benefit most from our hierarchic democracy and our capitalism and from the world of bad lives. Terrorism for humanity, say the one or two, would teach us a little more.

That is not my view at all. Terrorism, as a proper definition reminds us, kills or destroys immediately and much of it is unlikely to do anything else. Some of us have indeed learned something from September 11. It did teach us something, as hard lessons do. That does not justify the lesson or begin to. We would learn something, too, from terrorism for humanity. That would not justify it. You have heard my view, and it has not changed.

Still, let me pause. Something needs to be added to the proposition about September 11 and the proposition that terrorism to change the bad lives to which we have mainly attended, first of all those in four African countries, would be wrong because it would surely destroy more lives without a sufficient effect.

The principle of humanity, being serious and arguable, does not give an automatic verdict on all terrorism. It is a principle that takes account of the world in its differences. It struggles with facts and probabilities, with the difficulty of rationality. To my mind, still, it does issue in one conclusion of a certain generality, this being about *liberation-terrorism*, terrorism to get freedom and power for a people when it is clear that nothing else will get it for them. Struggles of this kind are surely special and less difficult cases. In them, a probable outcome has to do with what can seem to be the permanent resolution of a people to be free and the necessary moral weakness of an oppressor.

I myself have no serious doubt, to take the outstanding case, that the Palestinians have exercised a moral right in their terrorism against the Israelis. They have had a moral right to terrorism as certain as was the moral right, say, of the African people of South Africa against their white captors and the apartheid state. Those Palestinians who have resorted to necessary killing have been right to try to free their people, and those who have killed themselves in the cause of their people have indeed sanctified themselves. This seems to me a terrible truth, a truth that overcomes what we must remember about all terrorism, and also overcomes the thought of hideousness and monstrosity.

As surely, the state-terrorism and war of the Israelis against the Palestinians has been wrong. It has been an ongoing moral criminality. This has been unmitigated by talk of democracy defending itself against terrorism, with the terrorism self-servingly defined, in effect defined as what is done by Palestinians but not by Israelis. This talk itself on your television set, in aid not only of killing the terrorists on the other side, but of an extension of power and a seizure of more land, should be awful. To pretend that a self-serving idea of terrorism is just a plain and accepted definition is to engage in lying in the aid of killing.

Something related needs to be judged with respect to American support of the terrorism and war by Israel up to this spring of 2002, not concealed by mere speeches of protest and diplomatic visits and ineffectual pressures. America is *powerful*. It could have done otherwise. Something needs to be said too about the president's loose talk. There is also the matter of my prime minister's silence of behalf of America and its president, and his errands on their behalf.

But come back to our yet larger subject, the larger world of bad lives.

To go from the most to the least extreme idea of particular means of change, there is just voting. Well, it seems to me that our hopes of voting in our hierarchic democracies to help with the bad lives must be small. The Humanity Party isn't there to vote for. The Labour Party used to be something like that, but we don't have it any more. Nor will it turn up in America, if the past is a guide to the future, as a result of some limited change in the legislation on campaign funding.

Do you stubbornly have the idea, by the way, that we don't have to do anything personally because our democratic governments are doing something already? You're right that the War on Poverty is starting up again. Six months after the Twin Towers, Europe was promising to raise its aid to the world that dies early. We may increase our aid from 0.33 per cent of our national economies to 0.39 per cent. America may go from 0.10 per cent to 0.13 per cent. But you know, don't you, without my saying so, that this is nothing much, that it's tinkering at best? The War on Poverty first began quite a while ago, a long time ago. Our original pledge that all of 1 per cent of our Gross National Products would go to the poor countries in aid and loans has not been kept for thirty-eight years.

Each of us has the personal option of doing the useful thing of giving money to the right charities, in proportion to our incomes. We can do it despite knowing dispiriting truths about charity in general. One is that those of us who could give a lot, especially the corporations, don't even begin to. Another is that going on about giving to charity, particularly if you are in a government, is a way of avoiding policies that would be immeasurably better and would cost more than spare change. Charity is a refuge from obligation, something like Sartre's bad faith, not a solution.

Each of us could do more to resist the connected dispiriting truth that what we can give by ourselves, if useful, is less than a drop in the buckets that are needed. Each of us can try to resist, too, the truth that to give money in proportion to what you have is a kind of unfairness against yourself and your children. That is, you can try to resist a comparison between yourself and the persons and families around you. The better comparison is with the ones that are dying in those other places.

What is left, with respect to means, is maybe the best hope. It is what used to be called civil disobedience, which non-violence can be given new forms, new forms of non-compliance. To the credit of liberalism, Professor Rawls had a word to say for this sort of thing once, maybe even mass civil disobedience. It is not nearly as good as state-terror at getting things done, but it is a good supplement to voting, a necessary supplement. It is very likely better than almost all terrorism at getting truth heard, and in getting truth its rightful effect. It might get us something better than hierarchic democracy one day, and also gets us the results of better democracy.

Does talk of mass action or mass civil disobedience strike you as another of my lacks of realism? Could be, but there are some persons and things worth remembering.

There was Henry David Thoreau, who didn't do much, but got an idea planted in some American heads. He turned out not to be entirely out of touch with the world at Walden Pond. There was Mahatma Gandhi, who had a lot to do with getting independence for the continent of India by getting people into the street. Martin Luther King Jr also did something, and may one day turn out to have started more. There was the contribution of the students to stopping the war in Vietnam. There were those Germans too, including the clergyman whose name escapes me. Did you think they were a little silly sitting in that church in Leipzig with the candles and then processing around? Maybe they were, but they started work on bringing down a wall, did a lot to end an empire.

I've run out of steam, but not quite. There are two things about all of us on this earth. One is that we all have desires and needs. In my book, they are desires and needs for the six great goods. The second thing is that we're not all ninnies. Hardly any of us are, in fact. We can see through things. Those with the bad lives, to speak just of them, can see through the shams of our morality. They can see what we have done to them and what we are doing to them. So our question of what to do, and also their question of what to do – neither of these will ever go away.

A last word, implicit in everything so far, but recently in that plain speaking about our societies. What we need more than anything is a kind of intelligence. Moral intelligence. What we all need above all from Americans, on account of their power, is moral intelligence. We and they should see the need for escape from a lot of junk, a lot of morality with too many distinctions in it. We and they need to see how bad things are, and, in particular, how much they are owed to those of us on top.

Suppose you make it to one of those cocktail parties that some dream about, with famous people at it. You are about to meet the man who may still be spoken of by the *Herald Trib* as Mr bin Laden, maybe back from the dead. You are also about to meet Mr Blair, who has just agreed to do something about the state of the National Health Service, five years after he was elected. You shouldn't shake hands with Mr bin Laden. You could think about keeping your hand in your pocket with Mr Blair too.

Index

Index

horror *see* morality, horror in
humanity, crimes against, 126
humanity, morality of *see* morality of
humanity
human nature, 23, 30–2, 33, 153
Hume, 32
hypocrisy, 122, 124, 149

identifying with people in extremity
see extremity, identifying with
people in
incentives, 54; *see also* liberalism,
morality of humanity
income, 8, 14, 21
inconsistency, moral, 28–9, 148
inequality *see* equality and inequality
infant mortality, 6–7, 8, 21, 58
innocence, 85, 126
innocents, 7, 58, 103
integrity, 62
intelligence, moral, 148, 153–4
intentionality, kinds and degrees of,
78–9, 85
intentions, 78
intentions, morally good *see* morally
good intentions
interest-groups, 109, 113, 114
international relations, 59
intrinsic goods, 2, 4
Islamic countries, 8, 15, 21
Israel, 17, 25–9, 94, 150–1

justice 40–6, 46–51, 55, 62, 69, 70–1,
153; *see also* bad lives, equality
and inequality, morality of
humanity, right and wrong
just war, 128, 130

Kant, 62, 81, 90
Kerner, 31

killing, 54–5, 84, 89, 90, 101, 103, 118
killing and letting die, 74, 84, 89–90;
see also acts and omissions
killing, state-, 104
King, 153

labour, mixture of, 42, 45
Labour Party, New Labour Party, 11,
51, 60, 111, 149, 152, 154
legality, 35, 92, 93, 94, 104, 130
Leibniz, 10, 58
liberalism, 46–51, 70–1, 118
liberation-terrorism *see* terrorism,
liberation-
libertarianism, 40–6, 47, 69–70
liberty, 43, 45–6, 48; *see also* freedom,
moral rights, rights
Lincoln, 52, 106
lives, bad, 20, 30, 52–3, 58, 72, 121, 147
economic explanation of, 8, 13–15,
19, 21, 22–3, 131, 136–7, 140; *see
also* capitalism, capitalism as it
is, hierarchic democracy
good, 1; *see also* lives, bad
half-, 6–7
healthy, 8, 12
lengths of, 6–7, 8, 12–14, 16–20
lengths of, American blacks, 116,
136
lengths of, English & Welsh social
classes, 116–17, 136
our responsibility for, 85
quarter-, 16–17
wrongfulness of, 71, 72, 80, 82, 83–
4, 85, 87, 124
living time, 20 millions years lost, 19,
58, 123
Locke, 45
Logical Positivism, 122

157